Spirit Stones

To all my Elders, whose information
and guidance empowers my spiritual journey.
Blessed Be.

THIS IS A CARLTON BOOK

Text and design copyright © Carlton Books Limited 1997

A CIP catalogue for this book is available from the British Library

ISBN 1-85868-280-0

Project Editors: Kate Swainson, Liz Wheeler
Art Drection: Zoë Maggs
Design: Sue Clarke
Illustrations: Simon Mercer
Production: Garry Lewis
Picture Research: Lorna Ainger

Printed and bound in Italy

Spirit Stones

GROWLING BEAR IS
MICHAEL BROMLEY

WITH
KATE SWAINSON

CARLTON

CONTENTS

INTRODUCTION

'Our land, our religion, and our life are one.' **Hopi Indian**

Native peoples have lived on the continent of America for 30 thousand years, since Ice-age man crossed the Baring Strait from Asia and spread southward through the new land. They settled in communities from the Tundra wastes of the north, through the woods, mountains and plains, to the warm, lush lands of the southeast and the arid heat of the southwest. Each community adapted itself to the land, and honored it.

By the time the Spanish stumbled upon the Americas in the fifteenth century, the inhabitants of Turtle Island, as they called North America, had seen many civilizations both rise and fall. They were a population of about three million people, speaking many distinct languages, and had a rich and diverse culture, covering all aspects of trade, arts, crafts, and spirituality. They believed that the creative force – which some cultures called Wakan Tanka – created all living things to be of equal value, and that the spiritual ran through all of nature.

The Native peoples had an intimate relationship with their kin, all other living things, the spiritual world, and the land on which they lived. They treated all life – human, animal, bird, and plant – with respect, and managed the Earth's resources with sensitivity. And they gave thanks to the animals and spirits that ensured both their physical and spiritual wellbeing.

Using this book

This book outlines Native American spiritual beliefs and reveals how to incorporate them into your own life. Opening with a discussion of the close relationship that Indians had with nature and the spiritual world, it describes how they held animals to be sacred and harnessed their power through dreams and visions to guide them through challenging times in their lives. Theirs is a culture rich with spiritual gurus and vibrant celebration, and the book provides guidelines on how to conduct your life according to shamanic principles.

The significance of totems and the powers inherent in each of the animal totems, or spirit stones, are then explained in detail. You are shown how to use the stones to provide crucial guidance during difficult or significant times, and how to discover your own personal totem or guide is explained.

A final chapter discusses the different cultures who rubbed shoulders on the North American continent and describes some of the sites which they held to be sacred. Their traditional sacred history – myths and legends – act as a corner stone of all their spiritual beliefs and make more poignant the history of their dispossession of the land.

This book shows you how every aspect of the daily lives of Native Americans was filled with reverence. Use it to help you to understand the sacredness of your own life. Grasp it with both hands, and honor it.

NATURE AND SPIRIT

'All of creation is sacred, so do not forget. Every dawn as it comes is a holy event, and every day is holy, for the light comes from your Father, Wakan Tanka, and also you must always remember that the two-leggeds, and all the other peoples who stand upon this earth, are sacred, and should be treated as such.' **White Buffalo Calf Woman, quoted by Black Elk, Oglala Sioux visionary**

Most Native American nations honor Mother Earth because she governs all of life: living things come from her, are nourished by her, pass into her when they die, and are regenerated through her. Every living thing, whether human, animal, plant, or rock is equal in creation. Indians do not feel superior to animals; they are kin.

Their close relationship with animals is holy. For hunting peoples, animals consented to die and instructed shamans, keepers of the animal spirits, on the rules by which they should be hunted. Prayer and ritual were as necessary to the hunt as the arrow or bullet, for unless the animals were honored in the correct way they would not agree to be killed.

Everything that has ever lived is worthy of respect for its spirit is alive where its bodies is not. Each different species of animal has been created by that animal's Master Spirit, to which Indians pay respect by honoring the living animal before them.

The human ancestors gave life to all Indians alive at the present, and are therefore due respect. Native Americans have strong kinship ties with their living human relatives, and care for each other on a day-to-day level as well as in ritual practices and special ceremonies.

Spiritual medicine

All living things have a spirit, and all the spirits are connected to form a powerful spiritual world. The power of the spirits – medicine – may be harnessed to provide a range of spiritual healing. Every person has access to the spiritual world through dreams and visions, and they may consciously seek visions by attending a sweat lodge ceremony, going on a vision quest, or dancing themselves into a trance.

However, shamans and medicine men have special gifts to guide individuals toward the power of the spirits. Medicine men are a traditional and central part of native culture and spirituality, and have a strong effect on their community. They are responsible for healing the sick, dealing with troublesome spirits, guiding the individual toward their spiritual goal, and directing rituals and ceremonies.

Celebrating life

Ceremonies are an important part of daily life, celebrating the past and the present, bringing together a whole nation in song and dance. A nation may celebrate the rites of passage of its individuals, the coming of spring, and the renewal of nature. There is a wealth of rituals and ceremonies practiced over the North American continent, but they illustrate one common belief: mankind's oneness with nature.

Honoring the animals

'The animal hunted is sacred-power. So to follow his tracks one is on the path of power. To kill then the animal is to obtain power. All this is wakan.' Black Elk, Oglala Sioux visionary

In this painting by Joseph H. Sharp, Natives offer a prayer to the spirit of the buffalo. The shield decorated with drawings of buffalo, attracts the power of the buffalo spirits.

Nations based around hunting had an intimate relationship with their prey, on both a practical and spiritual level. For the Plains nations, the buffalo reigned supreme in their lives. They used every bit of its body: eating its flesh, making clothing and coverings from its hide, using its bones to make tools, even letting their teething babies chew on its gristle. Its habits defined the passing months, and it represented the good life. In the 1880s the buffalo was rendered virtually extinct by the white man, who would shoot it for sport and leave it to rot on the Plains. This was a tragedy to the Plains people: it destroyed their culture and their independence.

Hunting rituals

Indians honored their prey both before and after killing it, and many rites and ceremonies were practiced. Before a hunt or at the start of the hunting season hunters danced and imitated the behavior of the animal to encourage the animal to let itself be caught. After the kill they treated the carcass with reverence, thanking it for sacrificing itself in order to feed the people.

Some nations returned different parts of their prey to the Earth so that the animal's life force would return to the Creator. Shawnee hunters believed that a deer killed properly had four lives and would immediately be reincarnated. For the Sioux, hunting the buffalo in a holy manner ensured its return in future seasons. The rites assume paramount importance for nations in the Subarctic and Arctic where conditions are particularly harsh: some Inuit believe that when a caribou is killed its head has to be cut off at once to end the suffering of its soul.

Totem animals

A totem animal is one with whom an individual or group has a special relationship. The animal becomes a personal spirit guide (see page 39), affording guidance and protection to the people.

Many Native American families or sacred societies consider themselves to have descended from a particular animal, which assumes a pivotal role in their culture. Children are often named after the animal from which the tribe descended. Sitting Bull's name denoted him as an intractable buffalo bull, sitting resolute in the face of danger; he lived up to this name. Some individuals gained their special name after having dreamed of a particular animal and assumed it as their totem.

The Iroquois nation is divided into clans such as the Turtle

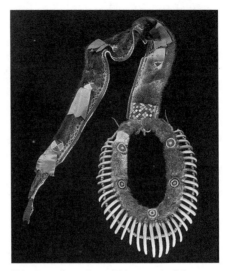

*Wearing a bear-claw necklace marked that a
brave act had been inspired by the Bear spirit.*

Clan, the Bear Clan, and the Wolf Clan. Perhaps the clan's
totem animal helped a human ancestor in some way, and a link
was formed between human and animal. Membership of a clan
is gained by individuals with the same totem animal: Buffalo
Society members of the Omaha tribe all dreamed of a buffalo,
and members of the Bear Society all saw a bear during their
vision quest (see page 40). The clans, and the individuals within them, assume the characteristics of their totem animal.

Fetishes

To harness a totem's medicine, many Native Americans make
fetishes of their animal. Many parts of the animal may be used —
bones, skull, feathers, claws, teeth, antlers — or other natural sub-

stances such as stone or wood. During their Midwinter ceremony, the Iroquois made representations of their totem animal from bone, stone, wood, or antler. Hopi Indians collected stones in the shape of their animal, and used them as grave goods.

For Zuni Indians, the most valued fetishes were stones resembling their totem animals which they often shaped to emphasize the resemblance. When hunting, the Zuni would carry a fetish of their prey next to their heart and breathe in its power at various intervals. At the kill, they would put the fetish next to the nostrils of the dying animal in order for it to breathe in the animal's spirit and strengthen the fetish's power.

Finding a name

Our name creates a resonance around us, it is meaningful, and says who we are. My birth name is Michael Bromley. My last name reflects my heritage: it is Old English for bramble-gatherer. Michael is one of the Archangels, so this name evokes a powerful energy to work with.

During my time in the US I met a Sioux medicine woman who said to me that I had Bear energy – not just because I am large and have lots of hair, like a bear. She said that one side of me is gentle and easy-going, and the other, which touches the fears and sensitivity of others, looks fierce. She gave me the name Growling Bear. If a person has the eyes to see past the obvious, the growling part, they will get to the essence.

Michael Growling Bear is one aspect of me. Over the years I have worked increasingly with Bear energy; I see it more and more in my character, and I become more accepting of who and what I am. Finding your own personal totem will take you on a wonderful journey.

Spirituality

'Sometimes dreams are wiser than waking.' Black Elk, Oglala Sioux visionary

Native Americans live in a deeply spiritual world, and express this by making every act every day of their lives honor the spirits, as well as by taking part in rituals and ceremonies. Some nations believe that the spirits take on physical form – as an animal, plant, or weather condition such as the wind. For other nations the spirits are powerful energies without physical form. Algonquian tribes consider there to be three parallel worlds: a lake underneath the Earth in which live the underwater spirits; the Earth itself, home to the spirits of all living things; a domain above the sky where live spirits of the upper world, matching those of the underworld. For other nations the geography is not so clear, but there is still a boundary between the present world and the spirit world. Crossing the boundary may be easy for people who have spiritual gifts or a characteristic that is appreciated by the spirits.

Dreams and visions

People are said to become strong and powerful when they have spirit power. One of the most important ways of achieving spirit power, and of great significance to most Indian nations, is dreaming. During dreams spirit powers come directly from the spirit world to the individual, without getting caught up in the physical world. Dreams usually need to be interpreted by a holy person, to help the recipient understand their significance. Dreams are so important in Indian culture that people who have dreams that

14

defy interpretation, or who do not dream at all, are considered to be cut off from the power of the spirits, and will not have a successful life.

Particular respect is accorded to dreams concerning animals, birds, or insects because they indicate that the recipient may have a special relationship with an animal, who becomes their totem, their personal spirit guide. Among the Sioux, dreaming of a bear indicates that the individual has the potential to become a medicine man, because the bear digs for herbs that are commonly used in herbal medicines. Dreaming of stones, rocks, or crystals indicates to the dreamer that he or she has power to bring healing or to predict events. Sometimes a song comes to a person in a dream; this dream song becomes a person's most sacred possession and is often sung at rituals in a sacred language.

The war chiefs Sitting Bull and Red Cloud were often considered holy men because their visions provided guidance to their people. Sitting Bull had three important visions in 1875, 1876, and 1885 (see pages 29–30); he and his people trusted his interpretation of his visions, and the dreams were realized.

Spirit guides

A spirit guide is a spiritual being that lives in the spiritual world, but who becomes attached to humans and is available to them as their helper and support. There are three kinds of spirit guide: a mischievous spirit drawn to a fearful or negative person, or to someone who is undisciplined in their spiritual work; a spirit who is drawn to an individual or group to guide, teach, or empower them spiritually through intuition or via dreams; or a personal spirit guide who is usually a previous incarnation. Each person may have many spirit guides, only some of which are revealed.

The vision quest

The most important dreams occur on a vision quest, a spiritual journey of awakening. An individual may go on a vision quest several times in his or her life, but normally when young rather than old since part of the aim is to seek spiritual guides for one's life.

Going on a vision quest requires special rites to be undergone. A person should seek the guidance of a shaman, clean himself internally and externally by fasting and bathing in a sweat lodge (see page 49), and receive a blessing. He then sets out alone for the sacred site where he spends time alone fasting and 'crying for a vision', as Black Elk describes it.

The individual hopes that the Great Spirit will bless him by sending a vision in which spiritual beings foretell the future, and in which birds, animals, insects, rocks, and herbs will offer themselves as medicine throughout the individual's life. After the vision quest a shaman often helps to interpret the vision that has been received. Any animals that have appeared in the vision become sacred to him, perhaps even part of his name, and he marks any shapes or forms he has seen on his body or clothing. The visions that Black Elk received on a vision quest were to reverberate through his life (see page 42).

Sacred bundles

After a dream or vision, an individual makes a sacred bundle, in which he gathers together objects which he believes will harness spirit power. A personal medicine bundle honors the particular animals which have spoken to a person through dreams and visions, and contains feathers, claws, bones, or teeth, for example, from that animal, together with wood, bark, or shells that appeared in the dream. Objects may be added as the individual

Painted on this shield cover is a bear with ferocious claws, untouched by flying bullets. The owner hopes to harness Bear medicine. Designs for such 'war medicine' were often received in dreams.

has further visions. A bundle is often hung behind the place where a person sleeps, where it may influence their dreams.

Bundles may be handed down from generation to generation, and contribute significantly to Indian culture. They may tell the whole history of a clan or tribe since they often contain objects that are said to have belonged to the first people. For many Plains and Southwestern people, a buffalo hide-covered shield, perhaps adorned with sacred objects or paintings of symbols from a vision, could attract the power of the spirits.

Black Elk

Black Elk, an Oglala Sioux, was a Native American visionary, well known through his book *Black Elk Speaks*, in which he muses on the spirituality of the Indian. He lived from 1864 to 1950, during a time of heated conflict with the white man; he witnessed the Battle of Wounded Knee, and saw the destruction of the Indian way of life. When he was nine years old he had a vision, lying unconscious for 12 days. The Horse of the Four Directions led him to a cloud where he saw the Six Grandfathers: north, south, east, west, up, and down. Each told Black Elk that he had important powers which would make him a holy man, and that he would show his people the way to survive. Black Elk then saw the suffering that his people would endure. The horse sang a song which was heard over the whole universe; it was so lovely that everything in nature had to dance.

In *Black Elk Speaks*, he says: 'It was the pictures I remembered and the words that went with them; for nothing I have ever seen with my eyes was so clear and bright as what my vision showed me; and no words that I have ever heard with my ears were like the words I heard. I did not remember these things; they have remembered themselves all these years. It was as I grew older that the meaning became clearer and clearer out of the pictures and the words; and even now I know that more was shown to me than I can tell.'

Black Elk would help his people survive by showing them the Red Road – the Indian Way – how to live in the modern world while honoring Indian values. 'The red road is a path connecting past and future, a road that is sacred.'

Using his rattle and drum, Hastin-Acani-Badonie, a Navajo medicine man from Arizona, chants for better health for both mother and baby.

Shamanism

The shaman is a skilled intermediary between humans and the spiritual world. He is responsible for preventing, diagnosing, and curing illness — not just of the physical kind but also that caused by witchcraft, violating taboos, or failing to respect holy objects. A shaman is able to imitate an animal's sounds and behavior, and communicate with it in its language. He may clothe himself in a bear or buffalo skin, and he is considered to become that animal.

Each nation has different shamanic practices and ceremonies. In the healing ceremony of the western Apache, a shaman tells stories to the assembled community about how the ceremony began. Then he uses his traditional tools of drum and rattle to beat a rhythm. The shaman enters the ill person's house, sits by the fire, and chants for two hours to summon spiritual power. For other nations, the curing ceremony consists of the shaman frightening away the evil spirits, then going into a trance and communicating with the spirit world. The most well-known form of shamanism is that of the Inuits, in which the shaman undergoes a spiritual journey on behalf of the ill person, or drums until the spirits come in and speak through him.

In order to become a shaman, a person has to receive a call to his vocation by way of a dream or vision, undergo a symbolic death and resurrection, acquire one or more spirits, and learn the secret language of the spirits.

A modern shaman

All journeys start with the first step. After a while, you find that each step is leading you down a path which you might not have expected to take when you first set out. This is true of anyone with a receptive mind and an open heart who explores the paths of spirituality. This is true also of my own journey.

I became a shaman many lifetimes ago, as a result of my own spiritual evolvement. As a young adult I rebelled against orthodox Western religion and, in travels around the world, explored Islam and Buddhism, among other belief systems. I then became interested in Spiritualism and received a powerful, personal message that led me to develop my spiritual gifts in a disciplined way.

My spirit guide

I was told in a vision that I had a spirit guide called Great Eagle, a Plains Indian. A psychic artist drew a picture of him for me which I still have to this day. I was disappointed at first that the picture showed him without an eagle-feather headdress. It was only later that I learned that such headdresses are worn only for war or on ceremonial occasions by great chiefs.

One day, Great Eagle came to me in a daytime meditation and said that he wanted us to go back to his homeland – Turtle Island. It was down to me to sort out the practical details, of course. In a few weeks I was in America, expecting to stay for a few weeks. I stayed for five years.

During my time traveling through America I opened a spiritual center and ran classes, workshops, and seminars to develop spiritual and intuitive abilities, as well as healing. I invited speakers and workshop facilitators to contribute.

How I became a shaman

It was through this work that I met Wallace Black Elk and Don Perote, whom I invited to contribute to my center. Wallace is a Lakota (Sioux) medicine man who was brought up steeped in the Old Spirits way. His spiritual grandfather was Black Elk, the renowned Sioux spiritual leader. Don Perote is Wallace's adopted son, a Potawatomi medicine man. These were the first shamans I had met, and I found that they had a tremendous impact on my life. Through the many talks and ceremonies we shared, they brought to me a change of consciousness that moved me from an English psychic's conservatism to the awareness of my own shamanic powers. The impact of my meeting them still reverberates through my life, even though many years have passed.

Wallace Black Elk and Don Perote asked me why I did not honor the spirit that I worked with and call myself a shaman. I protested. For two years I went through considerable soul-searching about who I am and what I wanted to do with my life, and underwent many initiations and vision quests before I could make the statement that I was a shaman. I am sure that the spirits brought about a transformation in me, which Wallace and Don could see. It was Wallace and Don themselves who revealed to me these powerful spirits, I am sure.

My shamanic path

I consider myself a modern-day shaman; I practice a craft that is as valid today as when it first began. My shamanic path leads me to teach, heal, and use my intuition whenever and wherever it is needed. Unlike most other shamans throughout the world, I have no shamanic lineage, no continuity of father-to-son teaching and understanding of spiritual teachings and ceremonies.

I call myself a Celtic shaman because the Celts were a very old and spiritual people who lived over a vast area including England. I am English and want to keep my own identity; I do not wish to pretend to be Indian. The only way I could honor my true identity was to go within myself and listen to the spiritual beings that are around me.

Ceremonies

'All Indians must dance, everywhere, keep on dancing. Pretty soon in next spring, Great Spirit come.' Wovoka, prophet of the Ghost Dance religion

Ceremonies play an important role in bringing together a nation, celebrating nature, and marking the passing of an individual's life from one phase to the next. There are different ceremonies, and styles of ceremony, among the many Indian nations.

Sun Dance

Many nations celebrate nature's yearly cycle. The Plains Indians hold the Sun Dance in late spring or early summer. This is a four-day, public show of dance, song, prayer, and drama, with some time for private contemplation. It allows people to renew their faith in the spirits, and was believed to guarantee the return of the buffalo during the coming year. The focal point of the Dance is a sacred tree, or a central pole with a buffalo skull placed on top. Everything is aligned east–west during the Sun Dance   a drum, sacred fire, dance sponsor, and shaman.

On the last day of the ceremony, a special dance involving self-torture may traditionally be held. During this, dancers are attached to the tree by thongs, tied to skewers which are pushed through the flesh of their torso. They endure a dance of several hours, at the climax of which they pull themselves free of their thongs, ripping their flesh. The self-torture and endurance give them powerful visions and are considered crucial to making the whole ceremony effective.

The practice was outlawed in 1881 by the horrified US, but traditional dances continued to be held in secret until the ban was lifted in 1934.

Rain-making ceremonies

The desert lands of the Southwest traditionally held rain-making ceremonies in late summer. In alternate years, the Hopi Snake Dancers, a sacred society, perform one of the most important and well-known ceremonies. Indeed, so many tourists and photographers thronged to the ceremony at the end of the nineteenth century that they threatened to overtake the proceedings, and were subsequently banned from the event.

The Hopi believe that the shape of the snake is related to the kind of lightning that precedes rain. For the first four days of the ceremony they go into the desert and bring back snakes. Then for two days they re-enact the creation of the world. After this they dance to show respect for the snakes in the hope that they will bring rain for the coming harvest. There is a final blessing, and then the snakes are returned to the desert.

Rites of passage

Birth, puberty, marriage, and death are marked with special ceremonies because at such important times a person is particularly close to the spirits. The most dramatic ceremonies are associated with the move from childhood to adulthood. For a boy, they involve isolation to mark his move away from his previous state, followed a test of bravery, endurance, or pain, before being welcomed into the new group. A girl who is having her first menstruation is usually isolated in the menstrual hut at a distance from

William Leigh (1866–1955) painted this evocation of the Navajo Fire Dance, which is characterized by vibrant styles of dancing.

the village and instructed about the taboos she will have to honor.

For Indian nations, marriage endures until death, and the marriage rites of the Hopi, among others, reflect this. In traditional Hopi weddings, the groom's family weave two wedding robes for the bride, one of which is to be worn at the wedding and the other kept for her funeral shroud.

Sweat lodge

The sweat lodge is a cave or specially constructed hut in which heated stones are sprinkled with water to give off a heat rather like a sauna. Sweat lodges were used particularly by Plains warriors for purification prior to battle, and continue to be used by men for spiritual purification before going on a vision quest.

The sweat lodge has much symbolism attached to it: its dark, warm, private interior is seen as a womb, from which men are reborn renewed and pure. The elements used are

A modern sweat lodge facilitator

Mother Earth is where all living things have originated and to where all things return. She provides for all our needs while we are alive. In addition, she helps us with our spiritual growth by revealing the many levels of spiritual energy that reside here. Going to a sweat lodge is understanding that by tuning in to Mother Earth and listening to her song we can perceive how special a place this is.

The sweat lodge has been part of man's spiritual belief system since he realized he had one. Throughout the world it provides one of the most common ways of going on a vision quest. As with all spiritual learning, the lodge has to be conducted with reverence and discipline, according to certain rules. It is part of the shaman's role to conduct – facilitate – them, and each shaman does this in his own personal way to suit his temperament or that of his particular totem animal. I have been a sweat lodge facilitator for many years.

The facilitator is accomplished in the rituals, and carries them out with care and understanding. It is important for a facilitator to be in charge because sweat lodges are powerful spiritual tools which have to be understood and used carefully. The ceremonies and rituals, which take place before, during, and after the lodge, are extremely important and complex, and require careful preparation and great integrity. If this is forgotten, misadventure or even death may befall the unwary.

I have facilitated at about 20 lodges, but do so fairly infrequently now because they are very demanding. In my experience few white men have the tenacity to withstand the transformation that occurs.

The purpose of a sweat lodge

A sweat lodge allows a person to let go of all the impurities on all levels of consciousness and to be open to the spirits that are drawn to the lodge, to see why they are there, and what it is they are trying to impart to you. Honor the reason why you have been drawn to participate in a sweat lodge.

The sweat lodge is a ceremony for men only – it is their special way of purifying themselves. Women have their Moon time, their menstrual cycle, which is their way of purifying themselves – getting rid of the old blood to begin a new regenerative cycle.

Inside a sweat lodge

A sweat lodge may be a hidden cave in a sacred place, or it may be man-made. Do not attempt to make your own: it needs to be constructed with the aid of a facilitator, and with proper regard to certain rituals. A man-made lodge consists of a hole about six feet deep and wide enough for about a dozen men to sit around the outside and half a dozen large rocks to be placed in the center. Branches are laid over the top of the hole, with either skins or earth turves on top of them. Inside it is pitch black and silent. The rocks are heated in a fire close to the lodge until they are white hot, and are then placed in a group in the center of the lodge. During the ceremony cold water is thrown onto them, creating an environment like in a sauna.

As the heat intensifies the visions become stronger. Each man leaves when he has had enough of the heat or when he has achieved his personal spiritual goal. One does not stay until the end in order to prove masculinity.

stone, wood, fire, air, earth, and water. These are basic to creation, and return the man attending the sweat lodge to his original state, close to nature.

Potlatch

Potlatch, which means 'gift' in the Chinook language, is a ceremony that involves the whole community. A family gives away, or even burns, a pile of goods – clothes, ornaments, tools, even canoes – in order to show their wealth and strength. Objects that depict totem animals may be given away as a method of transferring spirit power to the younger generation.

Such ceremonies are held to mark rites of passage and the transfer of power from the older generation to the younger. They include traditional singing, dancing, and sacred rites that show continuity with the past.

The Ghost Dance

In the last quarter of the nineteenth century, when Native Americans were struggling to hang on to the vestiges of their land and their culture, a new religion was born which promised them that their ancestors would return, all white men would disappear, and that Natives could live according to their traditional ways.

The religion was started in 1870 when disease killed a large number of the Paiute population; a weather doctor, or *wovoka*, dreamed that he had the power to bring back the souls of those who had perished. People were told to paint themselves and dance in circles. The practice flourished for a while, then fizzled out. Years later another weather doctor called Tavibo took up the reins, and his son became known as Wovoka, the reviver of the Ghost Dance religion. Under his lead the Ghost

Dance was not one cohesive religion, but a grouping of similar practices throughout the continent.

On January 1, 1889, while he was ill, Wovoka dreamed that he visited the land of the dead. He said that by dancing in circles Indians could meet the dead and reclaim their traditional values. Many Plains nations sent emissaries to Wovoka in order to learn about this first hand. Each tribe then interpreted Wovoka's message in their own way. Wovoka preached peace, but Kicking Bear, the Sioux messenger, related a more revolutionary message.

He preached that Wovoka was the son of the Great Spirit who had been killed by whites and had risen from the dead. A new world would come into being, all white people would be swept away, and the dead ancestors and buffalo would return. The people were to wear special Ghost Dance shirts, which would protect them from white bullets. The rise of the revolutionary Ghost Dance religion was of great concern to the US Army, who tried to disarm Plains nations. This led directly to the Battle of Wounded Knee.

Ghost Dance shirts were decorated with particularly powerful images. This one shows the powerful sacred character, Thunderbird.

In 1973 the Ghost Dance religion was revived by Sioux holy man Leonard Crow Dog who believes that his ancestors misunderstood Wovoka's message. He believes that the circle dance links the present with the past, the living with the ancestors, and is a way of keeping traditional Indian values alive.

2 THE SPIRIT STONES

'Each animal has its own Master Spirit which owns all the animals of its kind... so all the animals are the children of the Master Spirit that owns them. It is just like a large family.'
Raining Bird

Since the beginning of time mankind has wanted to find a reason for his existence. So he looked about him to see what he could learn and realized that we are but a part of a great universal plan that is unfolding every day. The Creator Spirit knows all that there ever has been, all that is, and all that will ever be.

Man started to reach out, to understand his spiritual heritage. He had a subconscious awareness that there was a spiritual essence in all things. He wanted to know how to work with and assimilate that knowledge in order to raise his own consciousness. Thus began his endless search to understand the Great Song.

Early man was in balance with his surroundings and paid reverence to plants and animals. His awareness of the spiritual aspect of all things around and within him began to evolve, and he developed an ability to interpret messages from the spirit world. In a modern, industrial, over-polluted world it is no wonder that humans are losing touch with Mother Earth and their own spirituality.

30

Sacred animals

Many animals are sacred to the Native Americans, having their own spiritual quality. Indians traditionally decorate their body, clothes, and homes with images of the animal, carry fetishes and sacred bundles to it, and let the spirit of the animal into their life to mould their characteristics and determine their actions.

This chapter helps you to discover and work with your personal totem animals. It discusses the role that 15 different animals can play as a personal talisman. It describes their spiritual and physical importance to the Native Americans and other cultures around the world. It then explains what the energy of each animal can mean in different areas of your life – your relationships with lovers, friends, and family; your physical and emotional health; your business, career, and finances; and your spirituality and intuition. You can help your own spirituality to grow and develop by listening to them, and letting them teach you to be close to nature and to your own spirit.

The Native Americans considered there to be different categories of creature, all of them people, just as we are. The four-leggeds include animals such as the bear, wolf, and buffalo. The winged people are birds such as the eagle, owl, crow, and raven. Creeping crawlers include the frog, snake, and spider, and the fish people are creatures such as the whale and dolphin. Man is a two-legged, of equal value to Mother Earth as all the other kinds of people.

To accompany the text of this book are 12 Spirit Stones, 11 of which have an animal marked on them. These stones are imbued with the spiritual power of the animals they show. The twelfth stone is left blank for you to determine your own personal talisman. Feel the stones in your hand, and become familiar with the power that emanates from each one.

bear

CONTEMPLATION

Bears and Native Americans have lived side by side for thousands of years, and to the Native Americans bears are the Grandfather of All Animals. Natives feel a particular kinship toward bears because they stand upright on two legs like a man. The soul of the bear is considered special.

Native Americans are impressed with both the power and fearlessness of the bear. Warrior tribes take the bear as their emblem, believing that his habit of digging up and eating roots and herbs makes them invulnerable in warfare.

In the culture of many tribes the bear plays a special role. For the Hopis the Bear Clan is the most important clan. For them and other tribes the bear is Guardian of the West, and Northwest coast natives revere the Great Heavenly Bear who guards them and represents the warrior spirit. In Inuit culture, the Great Spirit is a polar bear. The bear is a totem animal, sacrificed and ritually eaten by the Ouataouaks.

The Native peoples associate bears with shamans as both are considered powerful spiritual entities. The shaman, like the bear, serves as a messenger about future hunts because he is in touch with bear gods who are often hunter gods. In many cultures the shaman dresses up in a bear skin. The bear, like the shaman, is considered to have healing powers. Black Elk received bear powers through dreams visions, and considered that many of his powers to cure were granted by the bear.

The bear's habit of hibernating and emerging in the spring together with her cubs is a symbol of new life, resurrection, and inspiration. This natural cycle is often celebrated with sacrifice and dances such as the Grizzly Bear Dance.

World mythology

The bear is one of the oldest sacred animals known to man. Neanderthal man made altars to the bear and ritually interred its bones and skull with human bones. Classical mythology abounds with stories about bears, and the Old Testament contains many references to the bear as both a ferocious animal and a protective mother. In the cultures of Scandinavia, the Far East, and the Celts the bear represents either a virile power or benevolence and wisdom – both the male and female principles. Classical Arcadians and Mongols considered themselves to be descended from bears.

The talisman

Every year with the first snows that mark the beginning of winter, bears crawl into the Earth, the source of all life, and for half a year lie underground in a death-like sleep. In the spring they awaken and emerge with their young into a new world in which the Earth itself is being reborn. Their habit is rich in symbolism.

For Native peoples the bear's way of life represents contemplation and the ability to withdraw from everything, to go within to find the answers, to enter the silence of our being and evaluate what our dreams mean to us. Taking Bear as a personal emblem means that this is a time of listening to the spiritual influences that are trying to be supportive and to bring direction to your life. Bear is also the seeker of truth so trust him to guide you in your search for clarity.

Understanding the Talisman

Bear medicine needs to be treated with respect because its power is very transformational. In order to achieve what we aspire to we need to go within. This is sometimes called the Dream Lodge. It is important to silence the chatter within and without so that we can find quiet within, to ask for and be given clarity. This is the most powerful directional energy because all answers lie within us. Use your inner strength to vanquish all outer limitation, and be prepared for transformation.

Relationships

Bear energy is asking you to listen to your feelings and not allow outside noises to mask them. Make the time for this, for then you can move forward. But understand that when you evoke Bear medicine it will bring tremendous changes. Understand too that relationships are transitory and that we can learn from all of them – whether good or bad. That is what Bear is asking of you. Bear wants you to go within, to enter the Dream Lodge and ask for clarity in your life. But be patient, for answers are given in Bear time, not yours!

Health

Health is a state of ease, so if you are feeling stressed or unhappy you are in a state of dis-ease. You need to balance your spirit first in order to bring mental, emotional, and physical health. Bear energy is asking you to go within to bring discipline to your life. It is down to you and no-one else, for clarity can vanquish all fears, worries, and self-doubts. Bear is power, so use it!

Business

There can be great pressures put on us to succeed, to gain recognition for what we have achieved, and to grow rich. There can be a price to pay for this, however – emotional happiness, physical health, or just peace of mind. Bear energy has moved into your life to encourage you to go into Dream Time to remember what you really want out of life. You can get off the treadwheel and start anew. Be patient for the answers, and when you have got them, then just do it!

Journeys

It is important for Bear to feel comfortable in his home and surrounding terrain, for he needs space to contemplate and to nurture himself. If he is not comfortable he will move on. Bear energy reminds you that nothing in life cannot be changed. This is a time to re-evaluate your home life and acknowledge your restlessness. Now is the best time to listen to Dream Time. A journey begins with the first step. Take it.

Spirituality

It is easy to forget to listen within. You may feel a need to present a spiritual packaging that is acceptable to those around you as well as yourself. This builds up layers of ego and personality that belie who you really are. Bear medicine is taking you back to Dream Time to remind you that self-importance is of no consequence to those who seek spiritual awareness. If your night dreams are becoming powerful, keep a dream journal and use a dream dictionary. Take stock of what is evolving in a spiritual sense. You are being told things for a reason so trust yourself.

wolf

MENTOR

The wolf is a powerful symbol in Native American culture. She is a fierce animal who is loyal to the pack and protective of her family. Indian nations venerate her for her protective qualities – as mentor, loyal friend, and guide. Indeed hunters pray to the wolf to be told where game is, as the wolf has very acute senses and is able to hunt at night just as easily as during the day. Wolf songs that are taught in dreams or visions are thought to have special power, as is the howl of the wolf.

The wolf represents the Dog Star – home of the gods – as well as the guide to the afterlife. Indeed, legends of the Kwakiutls say that when a hunter dies he goes to the land of the wolf, and the Shoshone similarly describe death as the land of the wolf. Some nations claim descent from wolves. The Inuits have a Great Wolf hero, Amarok.

Wolves are wanderers and therefore know everything. This is a strength that warrior societies in particular want to harness. Indeed, Oglala war parties adopt the wolf as their emblem: they are said to be fast runners with great endurance, just like the wolf. For Oglala societies, and particularly the Wolf Society, strength through solidarity is their model. This comes from their observance of how the wolf operates in a pack. They also understand, however, that while wolves have a strong sense of their place in the family and the pack, they are individualistic and have their own character.

World mythology

By contrast, in world mythology, the wolf is usually seen as a powerful and terrible deity, a symbol of evil, destruction, and death. She is frequently associated with the raven, another traditional creature of death. Indeed, in Norse mythology, Odin is associated with both the raven and the wolf.

Yet in Celtic and Irish mythology the wolf is again seen in a positive light. She is claimed as the ancestor of one Irish tribe, and Cormac, a king of Ireland, was suckled by wolves and associated with them. Similarly, in Roman mythology, Romulus and Remus were protected and nurtured by wolves.

The talisman

Wolf has many admirable qualities. She is a loyal partner who mates for life, and has a strong affinity with the family unit. She is also a teacher, a pathfinder. The wolf pack has a complex structure of relationships, where each individual has its responsibilities to the others. The pack becomes a very strong unit and is thus able to survive.

The wolf howling against the backdrop of a full moon is a powerful image. The light of the moon represents introspection, in contrast to the light of the sun, which represents radiance. The moon is seen as the wolf's ally, and they both represent psychic energy and the creative force; both hold secrets and hidden understanding. The wolf baying at the moon is calling for that which is being shielded to be revealed.

UNDERSTANDING THE TALISMAN

Wolf medicine shows you that your senses are strong and that you have more understanding than you give yourself credit for. Wolf's link with the moon reflects your reservoir of intuitive and creative energies: trust them. Begin to share with others, for it is by sharing that we begin to grow. Express yourself creatively to help others understand you. Wolf often hides in shadows so find your power place, away from everything, so that you can work with the greatest mentor you will ever meet – yourself.

Relationships

All close relationships teach us about our ability to adapt and grow. At times those who are part of our life need to learn from us too. Wolf energy is asking you to be honest with both yourself and others about your relationships. Say what you really feel. Give yourself some space to see where true strength lies in both yourself and your relationships. Life has taught you many lessons, and Wolf medicine is showing you how strong and determined you are to overcome your problems. Allow Wolf medicine to protect you.

Health

Bottling up your feelings means that those around you do not really know you. You are also storing up serious health problems. There is a volcano of energy in each person; allow it a certain amount of flow since capping it will cause an explosion. Wolf medicine is asking you to express yourself honestly. Do not dwell in the shadows of fear and insecurity but come into the sunlight of opportunity and truth. Let Wolf see you grow into wellbeing.

Business

Wolf medicine is reminding you that you have a deep well of creative energy. Do not let your self-doubts and fears control you; use your natural insights. It is time to begin sharing new thoughts, expanding concepts that will bring you true prosperity and consciousness – the ability to have abundance in your life. Perhaps you have been taught a few hard lessons in life. Remind yourself of your strengths and resoluteness to overcome life's trials. This is a time of growth and development, so make your statement.

Journeys

This is a time to make a statement about your future. Journeys teach us most about life and the world. Going to different lands, meeting different people, and experiencing different cultures puts our own lives into a wider perspective and helps us move out of limited thought patterns. Wolf is very protective of her home, but has no problem in moving on when she has outgrown it. Home needs to be a place to shut the door on the world. Make it your power place, and use your creative side to make it a nest.

Spirituality

Wolf energy is showing herself to remind you to start questing for a new level of consciousness. Trust your instinctive thoughts and your inner knowledge so that you can expand and grow. Do not dwell on what you do not know but trust the things you do. As Wolf medicine awakens it will stimulate all aspects of your spirituality and creativity. Share this so that it can empower yourself and those around you. Let it become your teacher. Do not hide what you feel but begin to share, and see yourself grow.

buffalo

SACREDNESS

For many of the Plains Indians the buffalo portrays the most important of all the totem animals, for it was central to the physical survival of the pre-reservation people. They used the entire buffalo carcass for food, tools, clothes, horse gear, tipis, fuel, and in many ceremonies and rituals. In a spiritual context, the buffalo represents sacredness, plentifulness, and prayer. The buffalo is also thought to have supernatural power, and to represent the Whirlwind (see page 25). A white buffalo is deeply sacred, symbolizing prophecies being fulfilled and prayers answered.

The Cree, Sioux, and Pawnee call the buffalo Grandfather and Father of the Universe, and believe that he controls the way into and out of the world for the whole animal kingdom. In honor of his central role in their life and culture, many Indian nations celebrate Buffalo ceremonies and dances. These reflect the strength and endurance of the animal, and participants go through many tests to prove that buffalo energies run through them. Each man in the Buffalo Tribe of the Mandan Okapi must own the horns and hide of a buffalo and have killed the animal in a sacred manner. The men take part in an elaborate ceremony in which they perform rites and dances to ensure that buffalo be always plentiful and they be successful in the hunt. The dance reflects the range of a behavior that they hope to see from the animal during the hunt, from bellowing and stamping the ground, to the animal's gradual exhaustion and death.

World mythology

The buffalo has through time and across many cultures portrayed determination, strength, and power. The Bantu tribe in Africa honor the buffalo as their alter-ego. The Zulus believe that their soul can pass into the animal after death so that they can ensure that the tribe will not go hungry; for in honoring the buffalo the sacredness of the lifecycle will remain intact.

In Buddhism, the Buddha is sometimes shown as a buffalo or bull-headed. The Vedic god of the dead, Vana, rides on a buffalo. The buffalo was known throughout Europe, and in Roman times was seen in the amphitheaters in Rome. To the Taoists, the buffalo symbolizes the human spirit, starting as black and wild, and as the spirit is mastered, gradually becoming white and tamed.

The talisman

In the tradition of the Plains Indians, the buffalo is the very center of life, providing all their needs. In this way, honoring the buffalo is acknowledging the Great Spirit. When asking for help or giving thanks for that which has been given, Buffalo reminds us that we cannot achieve anything we consider of worth without honoring the Great Provider.

UNDERSTANDING THE TALISMAN

Buffalo medicine is about the power of using great strength in a controlled way, not only for yourself but also for those who are looking to you for direction. Recognize sacredness in every aspect of your life and everyone else's, even if it means unhappiness. Understand that everything is interconnected, a part of the Great Plan. Realize that only when all things are put into proper perspective are you able truly to understand yourself. The body has many gifts; understand that they are all sacred.

Relationships

Emotional change, growth, and development are part of the soul's journey. In a world where the trivial becomes meaningful, we lose sight of what our ancestors knew and understood, that all things are synergistic and all things are sacred. Buffalo has brought his power into your life to remind you of this fact. Honor yourself, for if you do not how can you honor others? Let go of people who are not honorable and who do not honor you, and replace them with people that honor you. Acknowledge them, for empowering each other builds a long-lasting relationship.

Health

Buffalo medicine is here to remind you that your health is a sacred gift. Your body needs to be taken care of for it houses your soul. What do you do to honor it? Exercise it, certainly, but also take time to quieten the mind, body, and spirit. Take care of yourself and those around you. Put things in perspective to bring balance and understanding to your life. Honor that higher idea.

Ask for help when you need it because it is empowering. Give help to others if doing so will empower them.

Business

Do not let money become your master; it is just an energy. Buffalo wants you to straighten out your priorities, to examine what you really want out of life, what you are striving for, and whether achieving it will bring true happiness. Honor every aspect of your life, and see the wonders of it. You will have gained nothing if you have not honored yourself and those around you.

Journeys

Buffalo has great strength and asks you to make a strong statement about your journey through life. Life is for living, so experience it rather than just drift though it. Creating change requires great determination and resolve. You need to be centered in yourself before you make your decision. Honor yourself so that you can move forward, particularly if the decision causes pain to others. Understand your motives for wanting to embark on your journey, and as long as they are good, travel on.

Spirituality

Power is a spiritual energy that is channeled through us. Buffalo medicine is very much about this. If you want to be a vessel of light then you have to be tested to see if you are strong enough. All things in life are sacred, and their energy connects all things. Understand this when you make decisions and you will empower yourself. Honor all aspects of the spirit, learn from them, and communicate them to others.

eagle

SPIRITUAL POWER

The eagle is of prime importance in the culture of Native Americans. He is the greatest, most majestic, most sacred of birds, and encapsulates the power of the Great Spirit. The eagle enjoys the freedom of the skies, and represents spiritual power and freedom, understanding, and spiritual wholeness. The bird carries messages between Earth and sky, and takes the prayers of humans up to the sun.

Shamans and medicine men consider eagle feathers to be the most sacred healing instruments, and only the most honored chiefs are allowed to wear a full eagle-feather headdress. The headdress represents the Thunderbird (see page 25). The power of the feathers is used in many healing ceremonies, but only the most revered healers are permitted to use parts of the eagle. Many Indian nations revere the eagle through dances, tribes, and ceremonies. The Hopi believe that the eagle holds both this world and the next in its claws.

World mythology

In mythology the eagle has been acknowledged worldwide. He is generally considered to be a symbol of spiritual power, goodness, pride, and victory. Since he flies the highest of all birds and goes nearest to the sun he is often revered as a solar bird. He is also a symbol for the sky gods, meaning that he represents the human spirit soaring to that which is higher and lighter. The Ainu of Japan consider the Golden Eagle to be their Great Spirit. To Australian Aboriginals, the sea eagle carries the souls of the dead back to Dream Time.

The eagle, as inspiration, is portrayed in conflict with the snake, which represents intellect. The eagle is always victorious for celestial energy always overcomes the limitations of man. At other times, the eagle is shown with a snake in its talons, in a simple representation of the victory of good over evil. In Greek mythology the eagle signifies courage and lives in the heavens. The Christian tradition has the eagle representing resurrection and victory over sin.

War gods, such as those in Assyrian, Babylonian, and Canaanite cultures, assumed the eagle as an emblem because it is a symbol of sovereignty and victory. For the Romans the eagle was the ultimate symbol of imperial military might.

The talisman

This is one of the most powerful of all energies relating to the spirits of creation. Eagle medicine is of power, strength, and inner awakening. Eagle's ability to soar high, to sit proudly, and to command power over lesser creatures is rich with symbolism in many cultures. The Eagle Spirit Stone harnesses this strength, this superiority, in a spiritual context. To be guided by Eagle means to stand apart and to believe in your own spiritual power.

Understanding the Talisman

Eagle medicine has walked into your life to remind you of your strengths, not your limitations. Eagle is bringing you a greater light so you can dissipate the darkness of fear and negativity in your life. It is time to take stock of your life, and move away from the 'turkeys' to begin the ascent to the 'eagles.' Let your higher wisdom and insight give you direction.

Relationships

Eagle medicine requires you to accentuate the positive and not dwell on your fears and limitations. It is time to strengthen your resolve; for those around you it is time to strive for higher ideals, to move away from the limitations of personality. Begin to visualize and let go of the past. Realize that power is given to be used for yourself, so that you can move along in your own life, and also to help the people you care about. Bring the light of clarity or inspiration into their lives.

Health

It is time to look at your lifestyle and see what is happening to your health – physical, emotional, and mental. You are strong – physically, and in your determination. View yourself in a positive light; do not listen to how others perceive you, or look to others to understand your own health. Eagle power has flown into your life to set higher goals for your state of health. Place your hopes, dreams, and ideals on a level that will set you free of limitations. Conquer the stress that affects your health; it comes from living a life that does not work for you on a spiritual level.

Business

There are ebbs and flows in our business fortunes, as with all aspects of the material world. When you are in a backwater of productivity, let go of conventional thought and help your inner self state where you are going and what you are trying to do with your life. Eagle medicine is about flying high, acknowledging your strengths and your ability to overcome obstacles. This energy is needed now – the capacity to reach higher goals, the elusive dream. It is time to fly there and make it a reality. Begin to open your wings and fly as high as your imagination will take you.

Journeys

Freedom is within you. Restricting your thought limits your ability to be yourself. Journeys are important. If you have never traveled, go in the mind to far-off places. Feel the freedom. At home get rid of the clutter and limited thought patterns to create a place of free-flowing energy. Remove the blockages to make your home a place where you can fly the dream.

Spirituality

While your own personality can be empowering and stimulating, at times it can be your greatest obstacle, restricting your growth. Eagle medicine has flown into your life to remind you of your high ideals and to help you attain them. Eagle is the profound healer, so acknowledge your own ability to heal yourself as well as other people in your life. He will help you to an inner awakening, higher wisdom, and insight. Trust your inner revelations and fly to the higher dimensions of thought, healing, teaching, creativity, and insight, for when you listen within all things become possible.

SPIRITUAL POWER

47

owl

PERCEPTION

Indigenous peoples of the Americas consider the owl to be the night eagle because it is silent and deadly in flight, and is a solitary bird with all-seeing eyes. The owl is generally regarded as a bird of sorcerers because of its association with – and abilities in – the dark. It symbolizes deception and silent observation because it flies noiselessly. The owl is feared by peoples who believe that the death warning is in its hoot.

In the Navajo belief system, the owl is the envoy of the supernatural world and earth-bound spirits. The Pawnee understand the owl as the Chief of the Night and believe that it affords protection. The Cherokee honor the bird as sacred because of its night-time vision, and wish to draw that power to themselves to see in the dark.

World mythology

The owl has a dual symbolism of wisdom and darkness – the latter meaning evil and death. In Ancient Greek mythology the owl was a creature sacred to Athena, goddess of the night who represented wisdom. The Ainu in Japan trust the owl because it gives them notice of evil approaching. They revere the owl, and believe it mediates between gods and men. The bird features prominently in Celtic folklore where it is considered both to be sacred and to have magical powers, again because of its abilities in the dark. Zulus and other West African nations consider the bird a powerful influence in casting spells, and think that using parts of the owl gives great strength to a person involved with magical incantations.

However, many cultures have focused on the dark side of the owl's symbolism. People have always been suspicious of the owl because of man's fear of the dark, or night, and those things that might dwell there. In general, the hooting of an owl is considered a portent of death or bad luck, and it may even prophesize death, as the death of Dido was foretold. It is a medical fact that most people die at night, and for that reason also the owl has been seen as the messenger of death.

In the Middle East, China, and Japan, the owl is considered as both a bad omen and an evil spirit. For Christians the owl traditionally signifies the Devil, powers of evil, bad news, and destruction. Similarly, in the Old Testament the owl is an unclean creature that stands alone as a figure of desolation. In an Australian Aboriginal myth the owl is the messenger of bad news. Yama, the Vedic god of the dead, sometimes sent out the owl as his emissary.

The talisman

The two main symbolic characteristics of the owl – its wisdom and its nocturnal activity – have made it represent perception as a talisman. Considering perception in a spiritual context, Owl medicine is related to psychism, occult matters, instincts, and clairvoyance – the true ability to see what is happening about you.

Understanding the talisman

Owl can see beyond what others can perceive; he has innate understanding and wisdom. When you have limited sight Owl medicine can help you see and understand what is there. Trust Owl medicine and work with it. You may be very restless at night or have powerful dreams, so keep a dream journal and use a dream dictionary to interpret them.

Relationships

Relationships are varied, and each one teaches a range of lessons from the simple to the complex. We at times see only those things that are at the end of our nose and wonder why we keep walking into brick walls. Owl has swooped into your life to remind you to stand back from your emotional life. Look ahead and trust your instincts if those around you are being negative. Deal with the problem. If darkness is in your life, let Owl medicine empower the instinctive light within and dissipate it.

Health

Fear, negativity, self-doubt, and vulnerability are aspects of the dark and can create dis-ease – emotional collapse perhaps or stress-related physical illness. They may also make you susceptible to other people's negativity. The demons of the dark have power over you only if you allow it. Owl medicine tells you that there is an antidote – to see things for what they are, not for what you fear they are. Owl is reminding you to use your perception to view things from a higher perspective, and then to begin to trust your own intuition.

Business

Some people take advantage of others, manipulate them, or give advice that is not supportive. These energies may be subtle so resist being drawn in. Strive to attain a higher level and watch what is happening, so that you can choose the right moment to swoop in to rectify matters. Owl is seen as the Night Messenger because he can see further than the obvious. You are being asked to visualize what is important to you, be aware of your own preconceptions, and see those around you for what they really are. Then swoop into action to resolve the situation.

Journeys

If you are feeling suffocated by your environment it is time to create change. Travel opens up new vistas, leaving behind limitation, bringing expectation. Journeys are never running away from but moving toward. You may be creating a self-perpetuating vortex of negative energy in your home. The only way to break it is by opening the windows, letting the fresh air blow away the cobwebs of despair. Redecorate, move the furniture around, get rid of the clutter, and let positive energy build.

Spirituality

Owl is the messenger of the subconscious. Look at the things that might be hurting you – people being unsupportive, critical, or jealous of you, or your own fears and prejudices. Using your intuition, rationalize what is going on in your life and trust your perception of the truth. This is not a time for hesitation or fear. Believe in your own wisdom or that of your own spirit guides, and move forward. This is a time for faith.

raven

THE MESSENGER

The raven plays an important part in the folklore of Native Americans as the most common Trickster hero (see page 24), a creature who both caused and protected from chaos, and who is responsible for bringing culture to the people. Called Big Grandfather, the raven steals the sun, helps recreate land after the Flood, and creates day and night. Perhaps most importantly, he is messenger to the Great Spirit. The shaman understands the raven as a shape-shifter, and it is usual for a shaman to become a raven in order to see what it sees.

Myths about the raven are widespread among the Indian peoples. The culture of the Northwest coast natives in particular is rich with representations of the raven. The Haida have a story about their origins, in which the creator-hero Raven finds a clamshell on the beach, out of which crawl the first people. Another story tells how the raven was originally white but, upon stealing fire for humankind, was burned black. This is a much more positive explanation for the change of color than is taken up by many other cultures, see below.

World mythology

The raven is a talking bird, and has always been feared and revered for the words of prophecy and wisdom it is believed to speak. Its ability to talk makes it the archetypal messenger bird. In

Greek mythology the raven is messenger of the Sun god, Helios, and in Norse mythology the god Odin has two messenger ravens, Thought and Memory, who fly all over the land and then return to sit on his shoulders and report back to him on all that they have seen.

In some cultures, the fact that the raven is black and feeds off carrion makes it represent darkness, evil, and destruction. The raven often appears with gods of the dead, alongside the wolf. The raven is the first bird mentioned in the Old Testament, cursed by Noah for causing the Flood, and represents desolation. Throughout the world many legends describe how the raven, originally white, grew black because of its noisy chattering and its need to be the bearer of bad tidings. Indeed, as prophets of bad tidings, ravens predicted the deaths of such Ancients as Cicero, Tiberius, and Plato.

More positively, ravens also protected Old Testament prophets and Christian saints. Zoroastrianism sees the raven as a positive energy because it removes the dead, as does a vulture, and so is a 'cleanser' of the Earth. In China, a three-legged raven lives in the sun; it represents the rising, the noonday position, and the setting of the sun. Celtic folklore has the raven as protector of warriors; and the Welsh hero, Owein, had a host of ravens with magical powers, who fought King Arthur's men.

The talisman

Raven has a very strong medicine. His blackness and habit of eating carrion place him in the shadows, yet his desire to protect and save are positive characteristics. Much complicated mythology has been created surrounding this dual nature. What is not in doubt, however, is that he has a powerful message to communicate – are you listening?

UNDERSTANDING THE TALISMAN

Raven dances in the shadows and has a powerful energy. While we think we are in control of our life, Raven makes the statement that there are deeper forces at work over which we have no control. Change will bring something very profound into your life. Raven is the bringer of tidings, a reminder of the Divine Plan that connects all things. Raven flies you into the realms of fear. Enter the darkness with him and see these fears for what they are: your empty voice of limitation. Listen to what the messenger brings you, then empower that message.

Relationships

Emotions are the best teacher about life. We try to understand relationships and deal with people in the best way, but people and emotions have a logic of their own. Trust your intuition, even if it tells you differently from what you want to believe. Raven reminds you of the things over which you have no control. Some call it destiny. Raven urges you to step into the void. He will guide you true, true to what should be, not necessarily what you expect.

Health

Health is a spiritual statement of your wellbeing. To have a healthy life at times requires change. To gain a feeling of wellbeing you need to start work on your physical health, for if bodily energy is low then it is not easy to raise energies on other levels. Raven energy is asking you to change your lifestyle, to step into the unknown. No matter how subtle the health problems assailing you, deal with them head on. Let the empowering begin.

Business

Raven has entered your life to show you that outside movement to your life is already happening whether or not you are aware of it. All change is good; whether or not you are prepared to accept it is another matter. Raven asks you to face change with courage. Fly with him into the darkness and see your fears as an expression of your insecurities. You can fly higher than your limitations. This is a time for profound change. Examine your attitude, take the challenge, and trust Raven to guide you true.

Journeys

To sell everything you own, jump on a plane, or carve a new lifestyle is not easily done. But unseen hands are at work, bringing change into your life. There is news on the way; either you create it or it will be created for you. Raven is a powerful mover, so to trust in his energy takes courage. But he can bring about wondrous events if only you believe. You are being told of them, but are you listening? Have clarity of foresight so that you can accentuate the positive in your life.

Spirituality

There exist both positive and negative energies. Negative energy itself can bring much positive change and transition. If you want to be a vessel of light you have to be tried and tested periodically to see if you remain strong. Raven will take you further along the path. He has no fear of the dark for he is keen of sight. Listen to the messenger, he is telling you about change. Spiritual work is a two-way communication, so make your own affirmation. You are part of the Divine Plan. Fly with Raven and see it unfold.

snake

CHANGE

To Native Americans the serpent, or snake, has both good and bad connotations. It is seen as an intermediary between gods and men, and may be either a symbol of eternity or a bringer of death. It is associated with thunder, lightning, and rain; the horned serpent, an enemy of the Thunderbird (see page 25), is believed to live in the sky. The snake is also associated with the fertilizing power of water.

Many Indian nations believe in the powerful role of the snake in nature. The Creek Indians honor it for its hunting prowess, and believe that it connects the hunter with his prey. Their Celestial Snake has a head but no body, and embodies all the powers of nature. Indian nations of the Southwest have a Horned or Feathered Serpent, a powerful water god who controls floods and earthquakes. The Kwakiutl Double-Headed Serpent controls all liquids, including blood and tears. For the Hopi the snake is a physical embodiment of the moon, the female principle, as both shed their shadow to be reborn.

World mythology

Of all creation, the snake is one of the most feared, loathed, and revered animals – and has a complex symbolism. It may be male (associated with the sun) or female (with the moon); represent both new life and death, healing and poison, good and evil. It lives underground, moves silently, strikes with a deadly bite, and can cast off its skin. It is considered to be in touch with the underworld, and is often considered an embodiment of dead people returned to the world of the living. In many cultures the snake accompanies Great Mother deities, and represents intuition, secrets, and enigma. In other cultures it represents darkness, guile, evil, and chaos.

In Ancient Egypt, as an aspect of the monster serpent Apop, the snake represents evil and darkness, and has power to induce thunderstorms, lightning, and whirlwinds. As Kheti, the huge speckled Spitting Serpent who spits fire at Ra's enemies, it symbolizes wisdom and goodness. Graeco-Roman mythology connects it with healing – Hippocrates took the form of a snake to save Athens from plague – and the dead, since the soul was said to leave the body in the form of a snake. By contrast, in the Old Testament the snake is a creature cursed by God; it was the snake who tempted Adam and Eve.

Throughout Africa the snake is a vibrant part of folklore. Many African nations see the snake as sacred, especially the python, which should not be killed. The Zulus believe that the snake is a dead relative who has returned, so must be treated with reverence. Many East African nations pay homage to the snake as either a spirit animal or a deceased family member.

The talisman

To peoples who live close to the Earth and understand its life-cycle, the snake represents the fertility of the land. Its ability to shed its skin reminded early peoples of the seasons of the year – of change and transformation. The snake, with its complex symbology, is able to protect itself with its bite, to be adaptable, and, above all, to shrug off its old self to emerge anew. It is these qualities that are harnessed in Snake energy.

UNDERSTANDING THE TALISMAN

When life gives you a snake bite, Snake power gives you the ability to rise above the problem. Snake energy is the power of spiritual growth, psychic development, reproduction, and sexuality.

On the physical plane Snake energy creates both passion and desire, birth and vitality. On the mental plane it creates focus, learning and judgement, direction and empowerment. And on the emotional plane it awakens both your day and night Dream Time, gives you determination, creativity, and zeal. When you let Snake energy into your spiritual self, you generate a re-birthing time, a final realization time, a period of greater wellbeing.

Relationships

You may feel the painful bite of sudden disappointment in relationships. But as Snake is a bringer of change, his bite is ultimately positive. Snake's other bite may be a new relationship: go with it and see where it leads. The best way to deal with Snake energy is to understand yourself through your sexuality, and to accept yourself. Snake energy brings fertility, so this may be a very fertile time for you.

Health

Snake's bite will create major changes. You need to know who and what you are, for the venom of the bite will make you re-evaluate your lifestyle, start from a new perspective. Snake medicine gives you the ability to change from the initial bite, to raise your consciousness and understand the powerful impact on your life. You may learn many things from Snake. His bite creates physical deep feeling, vitality, birthing, fire, and passion; mental understanding and direction; and an awakening of all deep emotions and empowerment of the Self.

Business

When Snake bites you may lose everything. This may be devastating or transformational, launching you in another direction. Snake brings a tremendous rush of positive energy and zeal to achieve. Sometimes a bite creates a turnaround in fortune, but other times the door to the past must be shut before a new one can be opened. Snake energy is about self-determination.

Journeys

Snake brings transition. Is he urging you to go on a journey? He is biting deep into all your preconceptions, fears, and limitations. That is why it can be so painful at times to bring change into a limited lifestyle. Snake energy also brings the ability to create change within the home environment, to begin the process of invoking what inspires you the most. Create a space that allows you the freedom to express yourself.

Spirituality

Snake medicine is bringing you a new awareness. With the snake bite comes the venom of change. Your consciousness will lift and a new life can emerge. Snake will awaken Dream Time in you and bring a greater perception of change. You will be able to let go of all that represents security. This is a re-birthing time, a time to begin to trust the spirits that you work with. It is time to make the statement that you are your own healer and teacher.

frog

PURITY

For Native Americans the frog represents cleansing, refreshment, purification, and initiation by water. The frog brings rain and represents the power of water. It is associated with Flood myths and is considered Lord of the Waters. The Hopi have a Water Clan, of which the frog is the totem, and they associate the frog with their cycle of maize growing, in which the frog represents the necessary water. The Lillooet tribe believe themselves to be descended from a frog.

In many shamanistic traditions, Frog medicine plays an important part in healing. The shaman places water in his mouth and, while focusing on Frog energy, blows it over a person who has attracted dis-ease into their lives.

Rain-makers beat out on their drums the rhythm of the bellowing frog when calling the Thunderbeings to show the essential life-force energy.

World mythology

Throughout world mythology, the frog is honored as a creature of the waters. She is a lunar energy, a rain-maker, who represents fertility and new life. The moist skin of the frog symbolizes rebirth, in contrast to the dryness of human skin in death. At the start of a rainy spell frogs come out of the ground in large numbers, making them symbols of fertility and the abundance of water.

The water deity of the Maya and Aztecs was a frog. In Celtic tradition, the frog is Lord of the Earth who has power over the healing waters, and the universe was traditionally supported by the Great Frog. The Ancient Egyptian frog goddess, Hequat, represented the power of the waters; she acted as midwife at the creation of the world and is protectress of mothers and the newborn. Frog was also an emblem of other Egyptian goddesses of fertility and birth. In Graeco-Roman mythology also the frog represented fertility. The frog represents the Chinese lunar principle, yin, and the Frog spirit brings healing and prosperity in business.

The frog has been an element in charms and magic for thousands of years. Frog entrails were used as charms in ancient times; medieval apothecaries used them in their medicaments; and witches introduce them as an element of magic in their brews. In magic circles frogs are whipped to produce rain.

The talisman

Water prepares and cleanses the body on many levels. Most importantly it is used to prepare a person for any spiritual work, washing away all limitation and negativity so that spirituality may flow unencumbered. Water is the element we understand the best, for out of the primal liquid we emerged, and from the fluids of the womb we are born. We were given tears to wash away anger, frustration, and hurt, and our saying that 'tears cleanse the soul' reflects this purification. Frog is honored for the purity that water brings; it washes away the unclean and in its place leaves a freshness that all living things instinctively understand.

UNDERSTANDING THE TALISMAN

Frog energy has hopped into your life so that you can take stock of where you are: Is your mind pushing you toward goals that your spirit is weary of? If you ignore Frog you will find yourself sapped of energy, lacking self-belief, or feeling negative.

It is time to reassess your life. Find your way to water to let nature's energies re-energize you. Otherwise, take a deep, relaxing bath with music and candles. Focus on all that is positive in your life, and visualize letting go of all the negative things. Call to Frog to wash away the old, to rejoice in the new.

Relationships

Frog reminds you that you are allowing your life to be as it is. If a relationship is draining you, it will bring you down. A sense of loyalty, duty, or obligation is just excess baggage. This is a good time to take stock of all relationships, for Frog is asking for the purity of inner thought. Make the decision to let go of non-supportive relationships and to strengthen those that remain. Let go and be happy for new and positive beginnings.

Health

Frog energy comes when you need to take responsibility for your own life. If you are strong-willed, stubborn, or determined, is this creating stress in your life? You are the one that is allowing it. If you ignore Frog, she will not be pleased. Act now. If you do nothing your physical energy will drop away and you will feel irritable, nervous, or tired. Recharge your batteries, visualize what you really want out of life, and then go for it.

Business

Perhaps you have been working toward a career and bank balance when Frog hops into your life. All your programming and preconceptions swim around you as you begin to review all aspects of life. It is time to re-evaluate your life. Who are you? Where are you going? What are you striving for? Clarity of direction is what is required. Do not underestimate the power of Frog, for if you ignore her it will aggravate a difficult situation. Frog says move forward.

Journeys

This is a time to re-align your energies by going on a journey. Frog is asking you to let nature start a healing process. When the body is stressed out, it is time to repair the damage, time to nurture, time to heal. Frog loves water energy. Head for the sea, river, or lake and let nature wash away the old and stagnant. If this is not possible then create an environment in your home that will help you unwind. Light perfumed candles, listen to music, and let your spirits lift.

Spirituality

When developing spirituality, it is easy to forget how to give without getting involved. The personality can become part of what is essentially a spiritual statement. Once you step over that line the ego can spoil other energies. This must be remedied. It is time to go back to basics, to find a space that is healing, nurturing, or therapeutic. It must give you privacy so that you can plug into the universal socket and re-energize. Once this process begins Frog gives you purity of essence so that that clarity can evolve.

spider

DESTINY

The spider is the most powerful creative energy to Native Americans. She represents the creator and the weaver of destiny. Indians believe that the great protector, Spider Woman or Kokyangwuti, was created to bring life to the world; she created the first twins from the Earth and then generated all plant, animal, and human life. It is often thought that the spider wove the web that taught humans the first alphabet, for she saw that man was evolving and needed something more than petroglyphs. The spider in nature has qualities which were thought to reinforce her status as creator: she rises into the air on a sometimes invisible thread, and she creates a web out of her own body, in which she catches her prey. Indian peoples are impressed by these powers, particularly in such a small creature.

The spider's eight legs represent the four directions and the four winds of change. For the Plains Indians the Trickster spider, Iktomi, is a shape shifter who also brought culture to the people (see page 24). The Hopi understand that the spider represents the essence of medicine, for she created this sacred gift so that honor could be given to all life forms.

The Oglala Sioux believe that weapons such as arrowheads and stone clubs were made by Iktomi, the Trickster spider, and that her web possesses power to protect from bullets and arrows, just as the web itself is not destroyed by these. They think that the web offers protection from thunder in the same way.

The spider is associated with womanly qualities – building a home and feeding her young. Indeed, Navajo weavers believe that they were taught their craft from Spider Woman.

World mythology

The spider is one of the most powerful creatures in world mythology and symbolism, and is usually depicted as a powerful feminine energy. In Ancient Egypt she was considered the weaver of the world, and in Ancient Greek mythology is an attribute of the goddess Athena as world weaver. There are echoes of this is Norse mythology too.

In Hinduism and Buddhism the spider is seen as the weaver of illusion as well as the creator. She was Vishnu's great weapon against his enemies, promising them whatever they asked for, then giving them the illusion that they already had it. For Australian Aborigines the Great Spider is the mythical Sky Hero, and for peoples of Oceania Old Spider is the Creator Goddess who made the Earth and the sky.

Spiders are considered a friend to man, and should be protected. Indeed, to kill a spider is to bring misfortune into your life. Healing potions and talismen often contain spiders.

The talisman

The spider is often called the Great Mother, the Great Spider, the Cosmic Spider, or the Great Weaver, and is the weaver of fate. She that spins the Web of Life influences all things. From her own body she spins the thread of life and attaches it to all people, linking them to her and the world. The center of her web represents the cosmic center, and the edges of her web influence the very web of time and the life and death cycle.

UNDERSTANDING THE TALISMAN

When one part of the web is moved the vibration is felt throughout the web. So it is in life: when destiny moves, every aspect of our life is affected. Some of life's lessons we think we choose for ourselves while others are dictated to us. Sometimes man gets caught in the web of illusion, so it is important to stay still and assimilate what is happening to you.

Spider energy is an extremely powerful creative force. It may encourage you to tear down your life to rebuild it anew, as a spider re-weaves her web every day. If the foundations are solid, however, you may build on them.

Relationships

Spider weaves the web of destiny. Touch one side of the web and the other feels a reverberation. That is true with relationships. The web of fate continues to move and change the lessons of life. The emotional self responds to many outside stimuli. When dealing with love, do not get caught in the web of illusion. Spider brings into your life the power to re-evaluate and redefine relationships. She may even require you to start from the beginning again, as she rebuilds her own web.

Health

Poor health reminds us of our mortality, making us take responsibility for our lifestyle. Do not feed on illusion or fear, but understand that the web of fate is instigating change. Spider is asking you to stand still and listen to your inner self. Begin to realize why you are not in harmony with yourself and the world about you. It is time to make a new beginning, starting from today. You can rebuild your life if you have the motivation.

Business

You have been striving for financial security, a successful career, or material ambitions. Suddenly the spider's web moves from a space that was totally unexpected and major changes begin. It is important not to get caught up in the web of illusion. Look objectively at the world about you. Use the creativity of Spider to begin to see what it is that you really want, even if it means leaving behind all that you have achieved.

Journeys

Perhaps you long to emigrate, to experience new places, to stimulate a side of yourself that has been dormant too long. Perhaps you need to find a new home that will help you be more creative and positive. Is it to be a reality of just some half-remembered dream? What is certain and what fantasy? Spider's web of destiny means that change is unfolding and a powerful influx of self-empowerment is beginning. So start anew or strip down to solid foundations. Spider is tugging your web, so be expansive.

Spirituality

Spider is pulling at the web of destiny, and changes are happening that you have no power over. Go with them, but keep your clarity and insight. Trust your spirits and watch the plan unfold. All aspects of your spiritual gifts need to be reassessed, and if change is needed then begin. If this is a time for development then welcome it, take time to adjust then deal with it.

whale

SINGING

For seafaring Indian nations, the whale represents part of the Great Mystery of the world and the sacredness of life. He is singer of the Great Song of life. Along the northwest coast and the arctic reaches of North America the whale flourishes, and plays a huge part in feeding and warming the people who hunt him. He has therefore become an important totemic creature. The Kwakiutls have a Killer Whale tribe, and the Tsimshian tribe has a Killer Whale Clan.

The Nootka, a powerful seafaring tribe based on the west coast of Vancouver, perform a dramatic and dangerous whale hunt, around which rituals and ceremonies have developed. The hereditary chief of the whaling community undergoes a preparation ritual for the hunt that often lasts several months and involves bathing himself, praying, and swimming in imitation of the whale. The whale hunters keep their camps clean and tidy out of respect for the whale, which is believed to approve of cleanliness. After the whale has been harpooned, killed, and brought back onto the land a ceremonial song is sung about how the whale is a man. The best meat is cut from the back of the whale and treated ritually. Choice pieces are later eaten at a feast given by the chief to honor the whale.

World mythology

The whale symbolizes the power of the sea and – because water represents healing and purity – regeneration. Throughout history the whale's huge size has given rise to many legends and beliefs. The jaws of the whale are traditionally considered to be the entry to hell, and the whale's belly is a place of death and rebirth. The Bible story of Jonah and the Whale reflects this.

Another ancient legend tells how a whale is mistaken for an island by sailors who land there and make camp; when it submerges beneath the ocean it drowns them all. An arctic and Russian tradition has it that the back of the whale supports the whole Earth and that earthquakes are caused by the whale's movement. For peoples of the Pacific – Polynesians and the Ainu of Japan – the whale is venerated as the mount for the god of the sea, or even as the god of the sea himself.

The talisman

The sea reflects the inner spirituality of man, and Whale symbolizes the Song of Life and spirituality, the essence of the Earth. Whale represents all knowledge and understanding from the start of time. A shaman who beats a drum is connecting with the rhythm of the Song for the drum represents the heart beat of man and summons the Great Elders of the natural world, of which the whale is one, to show us the path of enlightenment.

The Song reminds us of our spirituality. At one point in history there were so many whales that the Great Song could be heard on land, and with that reverberation man began to awaken his own spiritual potential. But now there are so few whales left that man is deaf to the Song.

Understanding the Talisman

Whale reminds you that you are a sensitive soul. He sings the Great Song: listen to its vibration and learn how to avoid the rocks of disaster and the storms of change. Every person has a natural intuitive ability. Let Whale help you to develop yours.

This is a time to sing your own song, to resonate to all that is true to yourself. Let that vibration dissipate all limitation in your life, and let your life's song be expressed so all can hear.

Relationships

If you become oversensitive things get out of perspective, your emotions are in turmoil, and your energies are in a state of disharmony. Whale reminds you that you have lost touch with yourself and the rhythm of life, that you are not resonating with the Great Song. Whale has swum into your confusion to remind you to take time for yourself. Breathe deeply, center yourself, and learn to swim with the tide until this learning time has passed.

Health

Tension, stress, pressures, and angst create frustration within. Whale is reminding you that your sensitivity, however great, will make no difference to the immediate outcome of the troubles you now face. You have lost touch with yourself so you feel the intensity of your situation acutely. Whale medicine is telling you that you must sing the Great Song. That means learning to relax, meditate, and unwind. Take up yoga or t'ai chi to remove the stress and tension from the mind, emotions, and body. This will allow you to resonate to the deep spiritual side within.

Business

Material energy can push many buttons within us – insecurity, loss of status, and the fear of failure. These fears are so intense that we lose the ability to be objective. By staying calm, however, you can steer a course of least resistance. Have inner strength, not outer susceptibility. Let Whale swim with you to the deep waters of your own inner understanding so that you can sing your own song. Resonate with it, let the vibration begin a clear rhythm of intent, and drown out the background noise of limitation.

Journeys

Running water is a great healer, washing away the negativity and restlessness of a life that does not encourage inner fulfilment and spiritual growth. Discover the place that can heal you, help you to harmonize your lifestyle, and find a new direction. It is time to make your statement. Whale reminds you that you have the ability to listen within, without your sensitivity confusing the issue. Find your own space by going on a journey or making your home a place where you can discover yourself, and listen to your own heart beat.

Spirituality

Whale sings the songs that teach man about his spirituality. The songs are in us but confusion, intensity, and dogma deafen us. If we are not listening, how can we be in tune with it? The Great Song of the Whale sings about the Great Mystery, and when we resonate with it we know where we belong in the universe. Whale medicine reminds us that we have a basic psychic ability. The more we work with it – in healing, intuition, teaching, or creative development – the more we can sing our true song.

dolphin

BREATH

The dolphin plays an important part in Native American tradition. She represents the breath of life, the life force, the rhythm of nature. As such she encapsulates the power of the Great Spirit. Owing to the fact that she is a mammal of the sea, breathing both air and water, she is considered a messenger between this world and the afterlife, a guide to souls in the underworld. She is a benevolent creature, in harmony with all creatures in the sea and on land, and is known and revered by seafaring Indian nations.

World mythology

The dolphin is generally considered a symbol of virtue, supreme wisdom, joyfulness, and playfulness – the most noble creature in the world. She is known as man's better self – more kind and sensitive than humans, and is said to have had human form until she took to the sea. For this reason there is considered to be a special relationship between dolphins and people, and she is known as the friend of humanity.

Indeed, as people have traveled the seas the dolphin has accompanied them and often been a savior, particularly to the shipwrecked. The dolphin is generally considered an expression of sea power and speed, and is often depicted with humans riding on her back.

The Greek for dolphin is *delphis*, very similar to the Greek for womb, *delphys*. For this reason the dolphin is often considered to be a feminine energy. The Minoan civilization on Crete took the dolphin as their emblem. In Roman art dolphins are depicted in funerary art, guiding the souls of the dead to the Isles of the Blessed. Egyptian culture associated the dolphin with Isis, goddess of the moon, whose tides wax and wane as do those of the sea. In Japan the Ainu acknowledge the dolphin as god of the sea.

The talisman

It is often thought that all that was spiritually positive about human nature left the land to live in the sea with the dolphin. Humans became corrupt over the years, but the dolphin was able to raise her consciousness to a higher level and remain in harmony with her surroundings.

Dolphin retains the need to breathe, and is in tune with the rhythm of the whole universe: above the waves and below. Dolphin and Whale both know the Great Song; whereas Whale is content to be the 'singer of contemplation,' dolphin is an extrovert and wishes to share with everybody the Universal Message.

UNDERSTANDING THE TALISMAN

Chatterbox has come into your life to remind you to take some very deep breaths. Center yourself, become grounded, and listen to the deeper side of your inner self. Find the direction in which you should be traveling.

Relationships

Dolphin has leaped into your life to bring a breath of fresh air into your relationships. Be free to create change, to broaden your vision, and to escape your programming so that you can grow. Take a deep breath and create change for those around you and for yourself. Dolphin brings much that is positive, caring, and uplifting into your life. Some of it is unexpected, surprising, and invigorating, so enjoy swimming in the sea of change, for Dolphin is your friend and helper. Remember to breathe, relax, and go with the flow.

Health

Breathing is the essence of our life, but how many of us do it properly? Most people breathe shallowly, using only the upper lungs; this tenses the stomach and chest, letting too much air into the head so that it becomes difficult to focus within. Dolphin energy is about deep breathing. Quieten yourself and stand calmly. Breathe from the solar plexus, slowly inhaling until the lungs are full and deep, and then slowly exhale. You will find yourself more centered, less stressed, with a new lease of energy, and with greater direction. Breathe the breath of life and feel the upsurge of positive energy.

Business

With the changes that Dolphin will bring, you need to be clear about the direction you would like your life to take. The business world is like a sea with both storms and calm periods: the unsuspecting may flounder or lose their way. Dolphin is coming to the rescue, to be your friend and to show you the way. She is asking you to breathe deeply, stay focused, and set a course that will see you in calmer water before long. Trust the inner voice that you and Dolphin can sing together.

Journeys

Dolphin has leaped into your world to bring you an inner understanding, a breath of change. The river of life takes us in many directions; sometimes the journey is through dark terrain, at other times to wide-open vistas. Dolphin is your companion through all of life's journeys. Listen within for the guidance she gives and you will find safe harbor. Make a journey if that will create a more positive lifestyle, or create a new home environment to stimulate a more tranquil or invigorating space.

Spirituality

Spirituality is the ocean through which we swim to grow. When we are in difficulties Dolphin is there to guide and remind us to be in harmony with our surroundings, as she is. If we trust and listen, then we truly have a spirit friend. Dolphin reminds you to take the time to breathe, to be centered and grounded within your spiritual development. She wants to breathe the Universal Song with you – to listen within, to take the power and responsibility, and swim freely in your own inner understanding.

twelfth stone
YOUR PERSONAL TALISMAN

The twelfth spirit stone has been left blank for you to choose whichever creature inspires you the most. Perhaps you already have an affinity with a particular animal spirit. If not, you may find that one of the four creatures discussed on these pages speaks to you.

To mark your creature on the stone use enamel paint or a permanent marker. You may use paint or ink to match the other stones, or another color – perhaps your favorite one – to signify the special, personal status of the creature on this stone. In this way, you can easily pick it out from the others if you choose to carry it with you as a totem.

Butterfly TRANSMUTATION

The butterfly symbolizes rebirth, regeneration, immortality, and the soul to Native Americans. The Hopi and other tribes in the Southwest perform Butterfly Dances, and believe that the butterfly represents a dead person's soul.

The mythology of the butterfly is largely the same around the globe. The change from a caterpillar to a butterfly represents resurrection, and in Christianity the symbol of the butterfly represents the risen soul. The emergence of the butterfly from the chrysalis symbolizes the soul leaving the body at death.

Understanding the talisman

Butterfly symbolizes our ability to transmute ourselves as well as the situations around us and even our lifestyle. Through each stage of our lives this ability allows us to grow from what is thrown at us by life's lessons.

Butterfly's medicine is related to the air or the mental plane. She symbolizes bright ideas and creative visualization. She also represents the ability to use colors artistically as well as to relieve stress or to become healthy. The sound of Butterfly's wings denotes change. Listen to it. It may be telling you to create space in your life so that you can grow.

Dragonfly DECEPTION

The dragonfly represents immortality and regeneration in much the same way as does the butterfly. For Native Americans it represents speed, activity, and the Whirlwind (see page 25). However, its unstable and shifting colors are an expression of illusion and change. In the Far East, it also represents irresponsibility and unreliability.

Understanding the talisman

'All that glitters is not gold' reflects Dragonfly medicine – that the appearance of things belies their true nature. There are winds of change on the horizon, but do not be fooled: just because something on the horizon looks to be of substance, close up it may be nothing more than a wisp.

Dragonfly encourages you to look into your life to see the illusions: your false perception of your body, your dressing to please others, the supposed path of your spiritual or creative growth, the illusion of other people's direction. Trust in the power of Dragonfly medicine to guide you out of this mystery.

Swan MEDITATION

To Native Americans the swan is a positive emblem of trust, the state of grace, and bowing to the will of the Great Spirit. To the Navajos the great white swan is a powerful creature who conjures up the winds from the four corners of the world.

In Hinduism the swan represents the breath, or spirit, and in Classical mythology it is considered a muse: indeed one legend has it that the soul of Apollo changed into a swan. The swan is also associated with love, purity, and music. She is often seen as a shape-shifter because she is equally at home in three elements – earth, air, and water.

Understanding the talisman

Swan medicine is of beauty and grace – and also tremendous power and strength. Swan is not be be trifled with, so have respect. Stand back and admire the grace and elegance. The polarity of color between white and black swans reminds us that in all things there are opposites – the yin and the yang.

Swan energy reminds us to make quiet time, time to go within. There are many levels of consciousness, from the mundane to the spiritual. It is time to go into Dream Time, for the revelations of things to come can be accessed with our intuitive ability. Jump onto the back of Swan and glide through the levels of awareness, and see the destiny of your life before you.

Turtle ENDURANCE

Throughout history the turtle has been revered as a sacred feminine power. She is considered to be Mother Earth, who supports and protects the world – both the land and the sea. The Native American name for North America translates as Turtle Island. In Sioux mythology, the world is a huge turtle floating on the waters; in another myth the world is supported by four turtles. Several tribes have similar myths: The Delaware believe that the turtle saved mankind from the Flood and now supports the new Earth that sprang up. The Pueblos celebrate a Spring Land Turtle Dance and an Autumn Water Turtle Dance in honor of the turtle. The Mohawks, Iroquois, and Algonquins have Turtle Clans.

In the traditions of Native Americans and other cultures the turtle is a Trickster (see page 24). More generally, she represents creativity, fertility, regeneration, and time. In many cultures she is considered to have supported the world at the beginning of time.

Understanding the talisman

Turtle is a totem for the Earth, connected to Earth energies. She shows us the need to honor the Earth that we reside in and from which we have come. This is a time for being grounded and allowing things that are hidden to be brought to the surface.

Turtle raced the hare, and because she was aware of her own belief system she had the endurance to keep going, even though others encouraged her to give up. Trust in yourself and persevere to achieve your goals. It might take a while to get there, but get there you will.

3 READING THE STONES

In life we sometimes need help to understand the energies that are around us. We sometimes find it difficult to decide how to tackle a particular problem or to see clearly what is best for us. Using the Spirit Stones will empower you and give you direction. Casting the stones and interpreting their message is a way of listening to the totem animals and interpreting how their particular guidance may be used to improve your life.

From the earliest times man has used different tools to help him interpret future events. Many years ago entrails or bones of animals were used. Nowadays astrology and tarot are popular. The Spirit Stones are in the same tradition. This book comes with 12 Spirit Stones and a Sacred Spiral Cloth on which to cast them. You may wish to buy or make a bag in which to keep the stones. Despite these tools, the ability of the interpreter is crucial for understanding the messages.

The Sacred Spiral Cloth

The cloth we use for the readings is called the Sacred Spiral Cloth because, when working with spirituality, there is a need to honor the sacredness of the event. The Sacred Spiral Cloth is an expression of this sacredness because it harnesses traditional aspects of Native American culture. The spiral has a powerful spiritual symbolism for many Indian nations. The circle is the most basic symbol of life for Native Americans. The sun and moon – perhaps the most dominant forces in their lives – are circular, and the pattern of their rising and setting is circular. Natives consider time to be a circle not a straight line from then to now. For Native Americans, birth, growth, maturity, death, and regeneration of all things – plants, animals, and people – is an ongoing process.

The spiral is a symbol laden with the Indian's most basic beliefs about life and the universe, and appears in many petroglyphs and early forms of writing. The Sacred Spiral Mound (see page 19) has a spiral tail, a symbol of respect and worship for Mother Earth. The Anasazi peoples in Arizona painted spirals upon stone to represent a sundial and would tell the time by it from the position of the sun upon it. For the Hopi Indians the spiral is symbolic of their migration legend by which they understood their existence in this world (see page 23).

The previous chapter as well as this one offer intuition in five areas of a person's life. The order in which these are discussed spirals in from our relationship with other people to our deepest relationship with ourselves. Relationships are discussed first, because these are perhaps dominate our lives; next health and business, because much of our time is spent in the pursuit of these. After these we come to journeys, and finally – as the center of the spiral – to our innermost spirituality.

Casting the stones

If you want to use the stones and cloth to make a reading about the direction of your life, you need to appreciate fully the seriousness of what you are doing as well has have an understanding of the spiritual forces you are evoking both within yourself and in the outside world. Before you start, find a quiet space either inside your home or outside, where you may be at one with

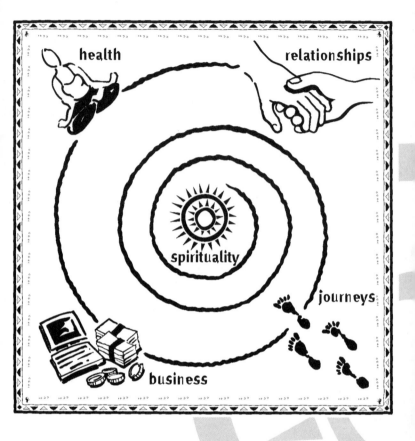

nature. Breathe deeply and calmly, focus yourself, and think clearly about the areas of your life in which you need guidance.

There are several ways in which you may choose to proceed. If you wish for detailed guidance, you may cast three stones on the cloth. Take hold of them in your palm. Clench your fist and bring your hand out of your bag. Hold your hand a foot or so above the cloth, focusing on what you are asking for, and then open your hand and let the stones fall onto the cloth. Take time to assimilate the powerful statement you have made. If a stone has not fallen clearly onto one of the five areas marked on your cloth, close your eyes and intuitively ask whether you should redo the casting or move the stone to the nearest area on the cloth. Whatever you decide is right.

If you wish, you may make a reading without using your cloth. If you require guidance during a defined timespan you may pick a stone at random and interpret its essence. In the five readings that follow, the individuals pick two Spirit Stones to help them through two time periods: up to one month and up to a year. If you have a more simple problem on which you would like guidance you may simply pick one stone and look at it to understand how its essence will help you.

Reading the stones

Once you have cast your stones, look at the interpretations for each animal on pages 58–103 in this book and make notes about what you think the casting is trying to say to you. Then allow your instinctive side to start work. Interpreting the message of the stones is up to you: there is no right or wrong answer that comes directly from them. They will help you to understand the energies in your life and will guide you toward the positive light of change. If a particular stone is meaningful to you, you may want to keep it about your person as a talisman.

On the following pages five characters with different life situations and problems cast Spirit Stones and make readings from them in search of guidance. The problems that face them are of varying complexity. By reading the thought processes of the five characters you will learn how to read the stones from your own casting and interpret them for yourself.

Rosie is in her late twenties, married with a baby. Her husband, Adam, has been invalided at home for four months following a road accident. He has not been earning during this period; Rosie works part-time from home. She is noticing an increasing strain on their relationship. While sympathetic about Adam's injury, she feels that he is intruding on her daily life with her baby and local girlfriends. Concerned about the family finances, she has to work more than she would like. Rosie is starting to feel isolated from her friends and is suffering from low self-esteem in every area of her life.

Looking for direction

Looking for some direction, she picks at random Frog, Wolf, and Dolphin from her Spirit Stones and casts them onto the Sacred Spiral Cloth. Frog lands on Relationships, Wolf on Health, and Dolphin on Business. She thinks about what they mean to her.

Frog and relationships

Take stock of what is happening in your relationships and understand that you need to say what you really feel instead of tiptoeing around major issues. Take time to sort things out in your relationships. You will find that clarity empowers not only yourself but those around you. See also page 86.

Rosie realizes where her relationship with her husband has started to go wrong. She sees, too, that she has been bottling up her own feelings because she has been wanting to concentrate on Adam. She arranges for a friend to babysit their daughter one evening so that she and Adam can have time together. They are able to let down their barriers, to cry about the accident and about what is happening to them, and to discuss how they will pull together until Adam is fit enough to return to work.

Wolf and health

Holding in what you feel only creates stress. This can make you restless at night when you should be sleeping, and irritable with those close to you during the day. You need to clear the decks and begin a healthier lifestyle. Learn to express yourself and nurture yourself. See also page 62.

This casting helps Rosie realize that she is exhausted – sleeping badly at night and racing around during the day. She has no time to herself and is becoming irritable. She decides to make time to attend the yoga class she abandoned when Adam had his accident. This would give her space for herself, time to relax both the mind and body, and an opportunity to spend time with her girlfriends. As Adam is regaining strength, Rosie asks him to share the chores to give her a break.

Dolphin and business

Either you allow yourself to become the victim or recenter yourself, breathe deeply, refocus, and decide on a path that will allow you to be more productive. Find a future direction for yourself that will allow you a more abundant life. See also page 99.

Rosie thinks long and hard, and realizes that she had been chasing her tail since the accident. And in the end nobody has benefitted. She doesn't know immediately how to resolve this problem but admits to herself that something needs to be done. In the short term she plans to go out somewhere relaxing the next afternoon with her baby to consider the options. She will then talk them over with Adam and come up with a realistic plan of action.

The journey ahead

In considering how to resolve the problems in her life, Rosie feels that she would like guidance for both the short term and the longer term. She puts her hand into her pile of Spirit Stones and pulls out Owl; he will show her the way over the next month. She dips in her hand a second time and pulls out Dolphin; she will be her friend for the next year.

Owl

Over the next month stop letting your fears and limitations keep building up. Use your inner strength and power to begin to formulate a new plan for the future. See also pages 72–5.

Rosie can see that she needs to throw light on her situation. Over the next month she will take herself in hand, talk about her feelings, try to understand what has been happening, and examine what she wants to do to improve the situation. She and Adam can see that he will not return to work this month, so they face the prospect of at least this period with no change to their situation. The change will come in their perception of the situation.

Dolphin

The next year is good if you can find the time and space for yourself to recharge your batteries and flow in life's current. Your own physical health takes priority so sort that out. Then you will see your energies rise in all areas of your life. See also pages 96–9.

It comes as a shock to Rosie to realize that she has been looking after her husband and baby for the past four months, but that nobody has been looking after her. That helps her to understand her negative feelings and her exhaustion. She resolves that once Adam is back at work she will take some time off to spend with her baby and girlfriends. If they can afford it, it would be great to have a family holiday to shake off the dust of their unhappy experience.

The open road

Casting the Spirit Stones helps Rosie initially to stop, assess the situation, accept it with courage, and actively seek ways to improve it herself. For the first month, she carries Owl in her pocket to give her strength and to enable her to see clearly. At the end of the month Adam is sufficiently healthy to fix a date to return to work. The family – and their friends and relatives – can start to see that the troubles are coming to an end.

Over the course of the year, Adam and Rosie talk about their dark days. They are able to understand the effect the accident and prolonged convalescence had upon their relationship, and they find that tackling the problems and improving the situation has strengthened their love and commitment. Rosie is enjoying spending time relaxing with her friends and baby, and each night when Adam comes home from work he sees how close his relationship is with his daughter and knows that he has to thank being at home for four months for that.

Sam, a businessman in his late forties, has been feeling vaguely dissatisfied with life for some time. He doesn't know for how long, but, looking back into the past, he can't remember a time when he was really happy. He is bored with his job even though he is very successful and highly paid, and he dreads going to work each morning. This sense of discontentment has been spreading to other areas of his life, and he often finds himself snapping at his family and feeling too tired to pursue his hobbies. His children avoid being with him, and his wife seems distant.

Looking for direction

Sam turns to his spirit stones for help. He closes his eyes and picks up Spider, Wolf, and Whale and casts them onto the Sacred Spiral Cloth. Spider lands on Business, Wolf on Health, and Whale on Journeys. This is how he interprets them.

Spider and business

Seeking job satisfaction, or contentment in what you do, is a priority. If your work gives you no satisfaction you will pay a price for it on another level. Fear can be a hard task-master. Follow your heart's desire and create change. See also page 91.

Sam can see how his negative feelings about his job are draining other areas of his life. His family relationships will not improve unless he tackles his work. He discusses the situation with his wife, Betsy, who helps him get things into perspective. Betsy suggests he take a few days off work to give him chance to spend time doing what he used to love – surfing the Internet. He feels fired by this.

Wolf and health

Health is as much a state of mind as of body. If you are not telling those close to you what you are feeling, how then can you fuel the changes you need? The first step is to be honest with your feelings. See also page 62.

Sam starts to understand how he has distanced himself from both his colleagues and family, and can see that he has been ashamed of his dissatisfaction, when ostensibly he is a success. He decides that the best example he can give his children is to be honest with himself and others – and never mind the example of a top-notch career. He talks to his children properly and asks them what they think he should do about his work. They are delighted to be involved.

Whale and journeys

It is time to take the holiday you have been promising, or just get away from the rat race for a while and move to a more nurturing environment. This is a powerful time for visualizing the future and for manifesting creative ideas. See also page 95.

Some of Sam's stress dissipates at the thought of a holiday. He consults Betsy and his children, and arranges for them all to go away together somewhere where there is plenty to do – and nothing – and an opportunity for him to go fishing. He remembers with a smile that some of his best decisions have been made while fishing. He hopes that the relaxation which comes flooding over him will help him to start enjoy simply living again. Then he can face thinking about the future.

The journey ahead

Serious decisions await Sam, and although he is feeling brave enough to take them he is slightly awed. He feels that he would like more help and at random picks Bear from his stones as a talisman to help him through the next month. He recasts the stones and this time picks Frog, who will show him the way over the next year.

Bear

Strive to find that space where you have a chance to get back in touch with your innermost feelings and needs. This is a time for inner contemplation and rest. See also pages 56–9.

Sam is relieved to have picked Bear, for he sees Bear as a big protective shadow, giving strength and succour. Over the next month Sam will give himself some space and time to think quietly and clearly about his life – about the life-enhancing aspects as well as the dissatisfactions. He won't rush his decisions; he will let them evolve slowly but, above all, surely in his mind. He and his family will take a holiday this month and, he hopes, overcome the tensions that have beset them over the past few months.

Frog

Let a journey bring you emotional, artistic, or spiritual creativity. Switch off the mind that keeps trying to analyze everything. It is time to re-evaluate all aspects of your life. Let go of the past and begin to build a future more in keeping with where you want to go. See also pages 84–7.

The mind that keeps trying to analyze everything; Sam can see that he will become like this if he isn't careful, and he resolves not to take himself too seriously. He thinks that he has two journeys to make over the next year: the first is his holiday; the other, he guesses, is a journey into himself to discover what he really wants to do with his professional life. He starts to understand the extent of this journey: examining what has gone wrong, understanding and accepting it, and then striding positively toward something new.

The open road

The process of casting the Spirit Stones and delving into his subconscious helps Sam to admit that he has lost his way, to accept this, and then to strive to find a new path for himself. He talks about his feelings with his wife and children, and can straightaway see that the family is starting to get on better together. At least he stops feeling sorry for himself and starts to feel the strength of his Bear. At the end of the first month, after the family holiday, Sam feels that he has found some peace and clarity.

During the next year Sam turns his attention to carving out a new professional life for himself. He finds that his interests and abilities suit him for a career in a field related to his own – being a consultant on the Internet – and he decides to learn as much as he can about self-employment and the possibilities of making a living in this new technology. He takes the plunge and sets up his own business, using much of the family's savings. Although success is far from guaranteed, he feels energized, challenged, and happy to do his best.

ennifer is at law school and has started to doubt the direction in which she wants her life to go. She feels that she has chosen the wrong studies and feels drawn to becoming a surgeon. Her boyfriend, Ian, who is working hard, is getting fed up with her doubts. Jennifer is trying to hide them from Ian, and is falling behind in class. She understands that studying medicine would require many more years of study, and is a challenging career. Would it be the right course for her? She is going round in circles and doesn't know how to focus herself.

Looking for direction

Hoping for some guidance, Jennifer pulls out Eagle, Bear, and Raven from the velvet bag which she made for her Spirit Stones and casts them onto the Sacred Spiral Cloth. Eagle lands on Spirituality, Bear on Business, and Raven on Relationships. Jennifer interprets them for herself.

Eagle and spirituality

Spiritual healing comes in many forms and there are various ways in which to work with those in a state of dis-ease. Do not let fears or limitation get the better of you. This is a time to aspire to what your insight tells you. See also page 71.

Jennifer is relieved: in Eagle she will find true encouragement and support. She is feeling betrayed by Ian and increasingly isolated and confused. For the first time she realizes that her gut feelings are telling her something important, and that she shouldn't deny them. She feels that she can start to rise above the problem. She also sees that the possibility of becoming a surgeon is real, and that she should consider seriously why it appeals, and think positive.

Bear and business

You have the choice about what to do with your life. Do not allow the pressures of others to push you into doing something that is not right for you, whatever their motivation. Live life on your terms. See also page 59.

Bear means self-assurance to Jennifer, and she gains strength from thinking she has the right to make a decision about her choice of career. She has been feeling like a victim; now she feels empowered. Afraid of what her parents might say about her possible change of studies, she hasn't expressed her doubts to them. She does so now, quietly and intelligently, and is surprised to gain their support for her now and in whatever she decides is best for her. She now feels free to choose.

Raven and relationships

Relationships, emotions, and feelings teach us many things, but the essence is that we have to be true to ourselves otherwise everyone else is living our life for us. Step into the unknown and trust in fate. See also page 78.

Jennifer has denied her true feelings to Ian in order to present him with an acceptable face. Their relationship is a sham – he not listening, she pretending. Jennifer feels afraid to talk to him about this, it would be easier just to pretend it hadn't happened. Yet this would not be true to her feelings. So she takes all of her new-found courage and makes a date with Ian to talk about their relationship. And if, when the air is clear, she decides that she wants to break from him, so be it. She would survive.

The journey ahead

Jennifer is starting to feel empowered and confident, yet she knows that she has a long journey ahead of her. She pulls out a stone – Buffalo – hoping for guidance over the next month, and a second – Wolf – who will be her mentor over the next year.

Buffalo

It is time to respect your own feelings and needs, and to break free from what other people want you to do. You are of strength and determination. This is what is being tested at this time. See also pages 64–7.

If Jennifer does not respect herself she realizes that nobody else will. Perhaps this is why her relationship with Ian has gone wrong. She has been so negative, so victimized, so whining. Jennifer resolves to talk positively over the next month about her desire to be a surgeon rather than complain about her law studies. She has to finish the academic term and sit her exams at Christmas. For if she gives up now and fails her exams how will she believe in her abilities to be a surgeon?

Wolf

Life is full of lessons that come both from outside forces and our own inner selves. One of life's lessons is that sometimes we have to assume the reins of our own life, to take charge. It is time to prove to yourself how strong you are. See also pages 60–3.

The next year will prove a great learning curve for herself, Jennifer supposes. She faces the hardest decision-making process of her life. Yet now that she is starting to feel stronger she quite relishes the opportunity to decide rather than drift. She has never thought of herself as strong – has hidden in the shadows of her parents and then her boyfriend. But now she has to stand up for herself, think for herself. She will keep her Wolf Spirit Stone inside her purse, always there for her.

The open road

Once Jennifer has cast her Spirit Stones she can feel that she has stopped falling and can start to assess where she is and how she will rise again. During the first month she talks to both Ian and her parents. Ian understands how strongly she feels, that she sees her feelings as an opportunity rather than an impediment, and that in the short term she will knuckle down to her studies. She gains status in his eyes. Jennifer understands Ian's feelings, and their relationship grows. Her parents are pleased to see how she is going to manage her life, and lend their support.

Once the exams are past and Christmas is upon them, Jennifer relaxes and ponders how to decide whether to change course. She talks to her tutors, other students, and an acquaintance who is a surgeon. The more she talks and reads, the more fired she becomes. She quits her course, having passed her exams, and spends two months doing voluntary work in her local hospital. She feels she has something to offer. The start of the next academic year sees her enrol as a medical student with recommendations from her former law tutors.

David, an engineer in his thirties, has been offered a two-year posting in his company's overseas office. He is keen to go because of the career and personal opportunities it presents. But his wife, Caroline, who looks after their two young sons at home, is not so sure. She has a circle of close friends whom she would miss, and fears that she might be lonely. Caroline is also concerned about how the children would adjust to their new life, particularly because they would have to find a school for their eldest son, who is now nearly four.

Looking for direction

Unable to see the situation with clarity, David pulls out Eagle, Whale and Buffalo from his bag, and casts them onto his Sacred Spiral Cloth. Eagle lands on Journeys, Whale on Relationships, and Buffalo on Business. David considers what they mean for him.

Eagle and journeys

Freedom is having the space to find your own individuality. To want both travel and a secure home life is not a contradiction but requires the ability to adapt. Journeys are a must: there is no choice, you must explore your personal potential. See also page 71.

David draws a clear message from this: he has been given a life-enhancing opportunity and should be glad of it, not troubled by it. He determines to make an effort to understand and accept the stumbling-blocks. He will listen to Caroline's misgivings and together they will consider what benefits they feel the family would gain by such a move. In discussion with his manager, David learns that a senior colleague from the overseas

office is coming over shortly with his wife, and arranges for the
four of them to meet up.

Whale and relationships

When love is involved, a difficult situation may become confused because the boundaries between our needs and those of others become blurred. Go with the flow until this learning time has passed. See also page 94.

Certain that if he weren't married he would jump at this opportunity, David is confused by how his wife and children fit into the equation. While he does not want to coerce them to go overseas he really does want to take the job, and quite relishes the chance to experience a foreign culture. He realizes that he has to avoid assuming that they will go: that would make Caroline feel unimportant and threatened. He loves Caroline and wants her to be happy. Although it is *his* job, it is a family decision that should consider everyone.

Buffalo on business

Is it worth the struggle to get where you think you are going? Are your goals life-enhancing and achievable? Only time will tell, but you need to be sure of what is right for you. See also page 67.

David breathes a sigh of relief at this casting: while it would be great to live and work overseas, and he certainly loves the sound of the project he would be managing, would it actually matter very much if he didn't go? The choice is his, and never mind the expectations of his boss. David also lights upon a new option: that he go alone. Although it isn't something any of them would particularly choose as the best option, it does offer a solution and is worthy of consideration.

The journey ahead

Having injected some insight into the situation, David now feels that he would like to be guided through the next month, in particular. He puts his hand into his bag and draws out Snake to help him in the short term. He does this a second time and pulls out Spider, who will be his friend over the next year.

Snake

Major changes in life always require a great deal of inner fortitude and clarity of direction. To do nothing will only create resentment and frustration, so change has to happen. Make it constructive, paint the big picture and go with the flow. See also pages 80–3.

David is starting to feel empowered by his chance to choose. He realizes that he has to face the decision head on, and not just accept with resignation to go – or to stay. He feels that over the next month he needs to try and work out what he really wants for his own life, encourage Caroline to do the same, and then see where their needs and desires touch. Perhaps she would be happier to stay here than move overseas. Perhaps he would be happier to go without the family than not go at all. And what about the boys?

Spider

In many ways you think the decision that you are making is so important, that it is almost a matter of life or death. However, as with all things in life, it is just another stepping stone along the pathway of life. Destiny is unfolding around you. Be part of it. See also pages 88–91.

If David accepts the posting, he will be there within three months. The next year will be crucial, both for taking the decision and then making it work. Just as there will be a start to the project, there will be an end to it, and then life will carry on. Spider will help him understand how his decision will fit into every other area of his life, both now and in the future. He will keep Spider as his talisman to help him see things truthfully and have the courage to reshape his life.

The open road

The casting helps David to gain a better perspective on his difficulty. He can now face making the decision, and feels confident that he will make the right decision – for the family as a whole as well as for each of the four individuals. It doesn't matter in the end whether he or the whole family go overseas, or whether David refuses the opportunity, as long as they are happy with their choice. After all, it won't be for ever. David feels able to say that there are many different ways to live your life, so why not this way, why not take up the challenge?

David decides to accept the posting and, in the first instance, to go alone. He comes home every month and his family come to see him for a holiday. Once Caroline has adapted to her husband's new surroundings she starts to imagine herself there and gains the courage to join him with the boys for the remaining 18 months. They decide not to put Kit into school but to let the boys attend playgroup, giving them – as well as Caroline – the chance to make new friends.

Miranda, a widow in her fifties, broke her leg nearly a year ago. It hasn't healed properly and she can now walk only with difficulty. She has had to quit her part-time job and has put her house on the market in order to move in with one of her children. Since the accident she has been prone to other illnesses and has been feeling very depressed. Her family and friends are rallying around her but she can't seem to shake off her black cloud. As soon as she thinks she is emerging from one bout of illness something else goes wrong.

Looking for direction

Needing help and support, Miranda pulls out Snake, Spider, and Owl Spirit Stones from her satin bag and casts them onto the Sacred Spiral Cloth. Snake lands on Health, Spider on Business, and Owl on Relationships. This is how she interprets them.

Snake and health

Major changes have hit you and it seems unfair that life should be so hard. The changes are asking you to re-evaluate all aspects of your life. Transcend the barriers around you and start healing by accepting the challenge. See also page 82.

Miranda's first reaction is to be cross: she doesn't want change and doesn't want to have to like it. Then she realizes that she has started to feel sorry for herself, particularly over the last few months, and that this has possibly contributed to her illnesses and depression. She sees that, through Snake, she can rise above the problems with her leg, the loss of her job and her independence, and her financial difficulties, and see the change as an opportunity to do something else with her life. Not to contract her life, but to move it elsewhere.

Spider and business

It is time to stand back and review what is happening, time to use the creative force to visualize what you want. Your fears will limit what is possible. What is your dream? Destiny has brought change into your life, so weave yourself a new web. See also page 91.

If Miranda is going to see this time as a challenge, she has to start thinking about what she really wants, not what her fears tell her she should be doing. Should she after all move in with her daughter and family? Or should she do something different? She could move to a smaller house or even sheltered housing. If she doesn't want to retire from paid work now she could do dress-making for a living, after all enough people have commissioned her over the years. The choice is hers.

Owl and relationships

Review your lifestyle with a new perception. Whilst the people around you may be trying to help, they may just be causing more confusion. Trust the intuitive side of yourself, and go with it. See also page 74.

It is time, feels Miranda, to look hard at the changes in her life, particularly at where she will live. Although initially she thought it sensible to move in with her daughter, she comes to understand that the possibility of this is actually causing her great unhappiness for it heralds the loss of her independence and the onset of old age. She knows that she needs to break free from her old way of life, however, and determines to think about where else she might live.

The journey ahead

Miranda feels that a light has shone onto her problems and she starts to feel that the ball is in her court rather than someone else's. She wants more guidance, particularly on what to do in the short term, and pulls Raven from her satin bag to be her messenger. In search of guidance for the longer term she pulls Wolf, a loyal friend to her.

Raven

Over the next month await some unexpected news or a response to communications. There is going to be healing in your life from outside sources. Transformation in your lifestyle is coming – welcome it. See also pages 76–9.

Miranda understands that while she should try and get control over her situation and how she wants it to become resolved, she should be open to outside influences. Perhaps she would win the lottery or her physician tell her of a new cure that will heal her completely. She necessarily can't foresee what the outside forces might be or when they might occur. For the moment she has to continue thinking positively about her situation, and bear in mind that she should be flexible, open to suggestion, and trusting.

Wolf

Life's challenges are on many levels and may be positive or negative. Whichever they are, you have come through them older, wiser, and above all else stronger. Use your new strength and resolve to improve your life. See also pages 60–3.

Miranda can see that she needs to regroup: to find some peace and space where she can consider the past year. In this way she can prepare herself for the coming one. She realizes that, like the wolf, although she has a large family with collective responsibilities, she is an individual and needs to think for and by herself. Once she has chance to get things into perspective she can start to discuss her situation in a new way with family, physicians, and employers.

The open road

Casting the Spirit Stones is the most positive thing Miranda has done for a long time. She realizes that she has come through many difficulties in her life stronger and more capable. This time should be no exception. What has been getting her down is that this problem affects every area of her life. Her leg probably won't get any better, but with a different job – or no job – and an apartment or bungalow she could probably cope. She needs to decide for herself how much independence she wants, and seek a way to achieve it. Miranda spends a week away with a female friend and feels energized by the end of it. In idle conversation her friend mentions that she is to take in university students next year.

Miranda now lives in a bungalow not far from the university and has two female lodgers who help her pay the bills, share the chores, and keep her company occasionally. She goes to stay with her children but is glad to return to her own home. Her leg has not improved, but she can get about well enough, and the pain has become simply an inconvenience.

CHAPTER 4 LAND AND PEOPLE

'Our land, our religion, and our life are one.' Hopi Indian *'I never want to leave this country; all my relatives are lying here in the ground, and when I fall to pieces I am going to fall to pieces here.'* Wolf Necklace

The North American land mass covers 2,168,930 square miles and, understandably, has a wide range of terrains, from deserts to arctic tundra, plains to forests, river valleys to mountains. It is vast enough to have comfortably housed about three million Native Americans in several hundred separate nations, each one steeped in traditions, rich in culture. For the most part they lived peacefully side by side, close to the land, in harmony with nature and each other – and with the spirits of their ancestors still among them.

They were bound to the land, as early cultures often are, because they depended on its bounty and beneficence for their very existence. The creatures that they found most abundantly in their land – whales in the Northwest coast region, buffalo on the Plains, for example – became their food stuff and their sacred, or totem, animals (see page 35), to whom they gave thanks and worship and who, in return, would protect them from starvation and evil spirits.

More than this, however, for their spirituality wove them to their landscape. This is the place of their ancestors; this is where they made their sacred sites. This is the best place to live in all the world, the very center of creation. This is the place where the Creator or the spirits intended them to live. This is where they were meant to be.

The people

Each nation has a special name for themselves, which is usually translated as 'The People.' The Apache originally called them-selves Diné (The People) but in the 1660s their enemies the Pueblos dubbed some of them *apachu* (The Enemy) and others *apachu nabahu* (Enemies of the Cultivated Fields). We now know these people as the Apache and the Navajo. Indeed, it was not unusual for the name by which we know a nation to have been given it by outsiders. The Nez Perce (Pierced Nose) were given this name by the French in place of their original Namipu, and the Lakota were in a derogatory fashion called Sioux by their ene-mies. These names have passed into common usage; indeed, throughout this book we use the name Sioux.

The land

The many Indian nations may be divided into separate cultural and linguistic groups, living in a usually clearly defined geographi-cal area. The map on the following pages shows the original loca-tion of some of the most well-known tribes, as well as the moun-tain ranges and the great rivers that act as natural boundaries between one group and the next.

The arrival of the white man, with his baggage of conquer-ing spirit, desire for progress, and disease did much to alter this picture. So too did the introduction of the horse into the

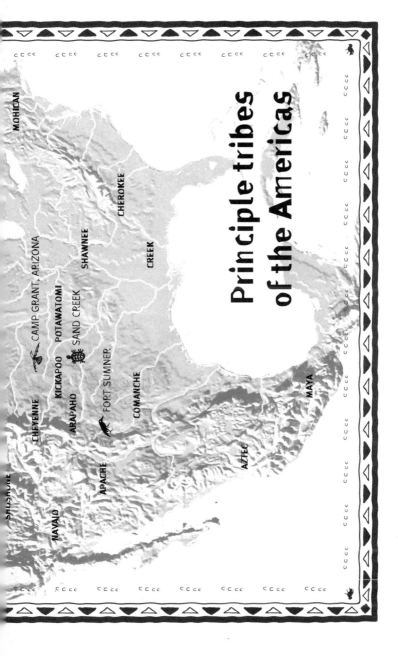

Southwest by the Spanish. Prior to this, the Plains in particular had been inhabited by hunter-gatherers, who remained in one place. The horse transformed their culture, allowing them to take to a nomadic lifestyle in search of the buffalo; however, it also allowed Natives from less favored regions to make inroads into the Plains in search of greater resources.

Arctic

The most northerly edge of the continent is the frigid tundra of the Arctic. Here the land is bathed in continuous sunlight in the summer and plunged into continuous darkness in winter. Temperatures are below freezing for nine months of the year, and life is hard for the few living things that make their home here.

Carved in the shape of a bird, this bowl is decorated with inlaid white seeds and red paint. It was made by the wood-working people of the forest areas of Alaska.

The Inuit (on the northern coast) and Aleut (on the western coast) belong to the same cultural group, and speak related languages. Both peoples hunt sea mammals, and the Aleut also catch salmon and octopus, and pick berries. Birds and caribou also sustain them. These peoples are bound to the land because they struggle to survive in it. They have a culture in which the shaman plays a vital role (see page 43).

Subarctic

This region covers the area south of the Arctic, from the Yukon River in the west to the south and east coasts of Hudson Bay. This is a landscape of lakes, forests, and rivers. A less harsh environment than the Arctic, the ground nevertheless remains frozen below the thin soil.

Athapascan languages are spoken west of Hudson Bay, while to the east the culture and language group is Algonquian. The population of this area is split into small family bands who lead a nomadic existence hunting, fishing, and foraging on the land. They follow the game, particularly caribou and moose. They use all parts of the caribou, which is central to their physical and spiritual existence, as is the buffalo to the Plains Indians. The people of the southern forests of this region also live on berries, roots, and wild rice. Family groups travel long distances to see each other and to trade.

Northwest coast

This region extends west of the Rocky Mountains up to the Gulf of Alaska. Although a northerly region, the people living here benefit from warm ocean currents along the seaboard and a large plateau of forests and grassland inland. Food, and particularly fish and sea mammals, is abundant, with salmon playing an important part in both their diet and their culture.

Tribes such as the Haida and Kwakiutl had an elaborate culture, building homes and totem poles from the abundant red cedar and decorating them with vibrant images of creatures such as ravens and whales. Inland tribes, such as the Nez Perce, were traditionally hunter-gatherers, living on fish, deer, and elk, and trading with the coastal tribes, until they acquired horses and moved east to emulate the lifestyle of the Plains Indians.

California

West of the Sierra Nevada, this is a warm, abundant, and fertile landscape. It was traditionally the most densely populated area of North America, housing over 300,000 people belonging to numerous cultural and linguistic groups. Most migrated here from other, less fortunate regions.

The people of this region were hunter-gatherers whose life followed a gentle and predictable rhythm. They enjoyed a rich diet of fish, small game, and plenty of wild plants for both food and medicine. They were forced from their homeland largely due to the influx of white settlers in the Gold Rush of 1849.

Southwest

Stretching from the Colorado River in the west to east of the Rio Grande, and south to Mexico, passing the Colorado River, this region is characterized by deep canyons and sandy plains. This was the traditional home of the Hopi, Zuni, Apache, and Navajo, among other nations. The Apache and Navajo speak languages derived from the Athapascan languages spoken in the north of Canada and Alaska.

The Apache led a nomadic live, hunting animals on the plains and picking wild plants. The Hopi and Zuni managed to farm the desert in a small way, exploiting all available living things, every drop of water, every spot of shade, in which to plant corn to sustain their lives. The Navajo people were hunter-gatherers until they acquired sheep from the first Spanish settlers; after this their diet and their culture changed, and they became expert, artistic weavers.

Central America

The civilizations of this region – Olmec, Mayan, Toltec, and Aztec – were sophisticated urban societies, which interwove the human, animal, natural, and spiritual into a complex tapestry. Hunter-gatherers at first, they grouped themselves into villages, farming a rich diversity of crops including tomatoes, cacao, chili peppers, beans, and maize. From these villages great cities developed, such as the Olmec city of Tenochtitlan, perhaps the greatest city in the world at that time. The Mayan and Aztec cultures were so sophisticated that they developed an understanding of astrological cycles.

The Olmec civilization (1800–300 BC) was the founding culture of the region, giving rise to the others. It is not known why the Mayan civilization collapsed, but much of its culture was passed to Native Americans (see Cahokia, page 20). The chain was broken in AD 1521 with the destruction of the Aztec civilization by the Spanish Conquistadores.

Great Basin

The desert between the Rocky Mountains and the Sierra Nevada, south to the Grand Canyon is the traditional home of hunter-gathering tribes such as the Shoshone, Ute, and Paiute. It is a rocky terrain with little water and only small game.

The Natives led a nomadic life as no one area could meet all their physical needs. The introduction of the horse allowed the Shoshone, in particular, to improve their meager resources by exploiting the Plains, and particularly the wealth of buffalo to be found there. The people of this region lost their homeland as white settlers came west to grow rich during the Gold Rush in the mid-nineteenth century.

This image of 1890 is the archetypal portrayal of American Indians. Living in their tipi on a reservation, some still wear traditional clothing.

Plains

This vast region stretches from east of the Rocky Mountains south to the Texas lowlands and east to the Mississippi. It is characterized by vast plains broken only by river valleys and mountain foothills. A few hilly spots, such as the Black Hills, the South Dakota Badlands, and the Sand Hills, standing out with extraordinary beauty, are considered sacred sites. This was a rich cultural region traditionally inhabited by the Sioux, Cheyenne, Arapaho, Crow, and Pawnee, to name but a few. So many languages were spoken that an Indian sign language was developed, understood by all.

Before the people acquired horses they lived in villages on the flood plains, planting in spring, hunting buffalo in summer, and harvesting in the fall. With the horse they became nomadic, full-time buffalo hunters. Native life and culture was dominated by the buffalo, who roamed the plains in their millions.

The white man destroyed the habitat of the Plains Indian in many ways: white settlement, warfare, disease, the near extermination of the buffalo, and forced resettlement on reservations.

Northeast

Down the St Lawrence River as far as west of the Great Lakes and south to the Appalachian Mountains, this region is home to the Algonquian-speaking nations such as the Ojibway to the north, and the Iroquois nations to the east and south.

The forests of the north were populated by peoples leading a nomadic life, hunters of deer and moose who had a strong spiritual connection with their prey, often considering these animals to be their ancestors. Around the Great Lakes the Natives had a more settled, agricultural existence, dominated by the seasons. The Iroquois tribes grouped together to form the Six Nations, considered the dominant Indian power by the white settlers who founded the United States. Originally a farming people, they dominated the fur trade based in that region during the eighteenth century.

Southeast

This favored region stretches from south of the Appalachian Mountains to Florida, and west into the Gulf of Mexico and the lowlands of Texas. The people here made early contact with Spanish settlers and did much to accommodate them. The Choctaw, Chicasaw, Creek, Cherokee, and Seminole nations became known as the Five Civilized Tribes.

With a warm, wet climate, the region is rich in both plants and animals. The people are farmers, cultivating maize, bananas, and sugar cane, as well as tobacco and herbs for use in rituals.

Sacred sites

'The earth and myself are of one mind.'
Chief Joseph, Nez Perce

Throughout North America there are many sites sacred to Native Americans. These special places are an integral part of the landscape, and here people feel particularly close to their spirits – especially the Great Spirit, their creator. High ground is often considered the most sacred land because it seems to reach up through the sky to the spirits. For some Northwest coast peoples certain beaches are considered sacred: the meeting place between the spirits of the land and those of the sea. Stones or shells taken from such beaches are considered to harness the protective qualities of the spirits.

Chaco Canyon

Described as an ancient apartment block, Chaco Canyon in Mexico was home to the Anasazi – the Ancient Ones, ancestors of the Hopi and Zuni – from a few centuries BC up to the twelfth century AD. The largest town in Chaco Canyon is called Pueblo Bonito, Beautiful Village, and extends over 3 acres. It became a major industrial center for trade in turquoise.

The town was built in a semi-circle, with a multistory complex of 700 rooms facing the central plaza. Underneath the plaza are two large, circular chambers, *kivas*, which were used to hold ceremonies for men only. In the center of the *kiva*'s floor is a recess called the *sipapu*; this symbolizes the hole through which the first people were said to emerge into the world, according to the Hopi creation story (see page 23).

The undulating, green curves of the Great Serpent Mound in Adams County, Ohio, are one of the most enduring images of Native America. The simple beauty and spiritual significance of the Mound led early anthropologists to recognize the sophisticated culture of the Indian.

The Great Serpent Mound

This man-made earthwork in Ohio is one of the most striking and well-known Indian sites. Over 1,200 feet long and 5 feet high, it takes the form of a snake with an egg or a frog in its mouth. Its tail is coiled in a spiral, a familiar symbol of the sacred forces of the Earth (see also Sacred Spiral Cloth, page 104).

It is probable that the Mound was built between the sixth and first centuries BC by the Adena people, hunters and foragers, whose remains have been found in the area. Anthropologists consider that it was built to provide a platform for ceremonies or for use as a sacred platform, rather than as a burial mound.

The Mound may be seen properly only from above, which suggests that it was intended as a signal to the Great Spirit in the sky. The shape of the serpent, together with its egg-shape and coiled tail, also seem to signify that the Natives who built it worshiped the Earth as their divine mother.

Cahokia

Just outside St Louis, Missouri, on the banks of the Mississippi, Cahokia is a collection of over 200 flat-topped pyramids and earth mounds, reminiscent of Mayan pyramids. Covering 5 square miles, it was a city and ceremonial center at its peak of use between AD 1050 and 1250. At this time Cahokia was the most sophisticated urban center north of Mexico.

The sacred center of the city is Monk's Mound, on top of which was a wooden structure 100 feet high, in which lived the priest. The city's population of 10,000 or so lived in wooden houses at the feet of the mounds.

Of particular interest has been the discovery that the mounds themselves and a ring of stakes are aligned in a way that suggests they were used as a solar calendar to determine the dates of ceremonies and festivals.

Bighorn medicine wheel

There are many medicine wheels in North America. The best known one is probably the Bighorn medicine wheel in Wyoming, nearly 10,000 feet above sea level on the shoulder of the Bighorn Mountains. Small boulders have been positioned to form a wheel over 100 feet in diameter. At its hub is a cairn (pile of stones), with six cairns around its circumference, and 28 lines of stones forming spokes radiating from the center. Anthropologists suppose that one of the northern Plains tribes – the Arapaho, Cheyenne, or Crow – built it.

The hub and one protruding cairn are aligned with the position of the sun at dawn on Midsummer's Day, suggesting that the wheel was used to create an annual calendar or to determine particularly important dates. Perhaps, more simply, it symbolizes the sacredness of the Earth, represents the Indian notion of time as a circle, or serves to connect the people with the land and the spirits. It would certainly have been used as a place of prayer and vision quests. As part of a network of medicine wheels built on high ground, it may have acted as a beacon for nomadic peoples.

The Peterborough petroglyphs

Near Stony Lake in Peterborough, Ontario, this site is sacred to the Ojibway, who call it Kinomagewapkong, 'The Rocks That Teach.' The site is 180 feet long and 100 feet wide, and consists of over 900 images of humans, animals, and objects carved onto a huge outcrop of white, crystalline limestone. They were carved by the Algonquian people between AD 900 and 1400.

Among the largest petroglyphs are a solar figure (or shaman), who has above his head a radiant sun, and a boat that looks very much like a Viking ship. These carvings have sacred meaning. On this site there are also many carvings of the turtle, which was one of the most sacred animals to the Algonquians.

This carving may show a person receiving power from the heavens, or the Great Spirit of the Algonquians – Kitchi Manitou.

A natural phenomenon occurs in the springtime, which contributes to the sacredness of this site: through deep holes in the rock that have been caused by the elements rise eerie noises from underground, as if the spirits of the underworld were talking.

Sacred history

'I did not come here. I was put here by the Creator.'
Yakima Indian

The sacred history of Native Americans recalls the creation of the Earth and the origins of the people. Each nation has its own stories, using familiar characters and settings from their own land. The stories are vibrant, rich in symbolism and spirituality, and filled with people, animals, and supernatural beings. The stories are considered to be true – unlike myths, which are generally regarded as symbolic versions of events.

Sacred history is an oral tradition, retold at ceremonies and passed on from generation to generation. The stories are living history as they exist in countless versions, changing slightly in each retelling to incorporate details of the narrator's own dreams (see page 38) or interpretations. They are also carried on in songs and dances, where they become an important part of ceremonies (see page 47).

Origin and creation stories

Most origin stories show how close the relationship is between people, animals, the land, the spirits, and the creator. It was the creator himself – variously called Wakan Tanka, the Great Spirit, the Master of Life – who breathed life into humans and connected their spirits with those of all other livings things in the universe. He sited the tribe on their own land at the beginning of time so that a bond could be created between humans and their landscape. Indeed, most nations consider that their homeland bears the scars of their birth to remind the people of their origins.

In the Southwest, descendants of the Anasazi people – the Hopi and Zuni – have stories of how people emerged from under the Earth at precise places in the landscape. These stories reflect their lifestyle as farmers settled on the land. According to Hopi tradition, the first people traveled upward through three worlds before they reached this world. Their spirit guide, Másaw, then instructed them to travel north, south, east, and west until they came to the sea, and then to retrace their steps home. The *kivas* at Chaco Canyon preserve the memory of this event (see page 18). The Navajo story similarly tells of upward migration through three worlds.

In contrast, the origin and creation stories of less geographically settled hunter-gathering nations are dominated by their traditional quarry. Tribes of the mountainous Northwest, including the Nez Perce, tell of a time when the world was inhabited by animals alone, who had human characteristics and spoke like humans. A fierce monster terrified all the animals, caught them, and devoured them. A coyote culture hero (see page 24) jumped inside the monster and cut up his heart before chopping him into small pieces, creating a different tribe from each part. Each tribe considers that they came from the monster's heart, making them the bravest and wisest tribe.

Many hunter-gatherering nations have stories telling how the Earth was created without form or feature before the intervention of an earthdiver. In these stories, the Earth consists of water alone, with no dry land. A supernatural being – perhaps the Great Spirit – asks various animals to dive to the bottom of the water in order to bring up mud and create land. One creature succeeds in this. This animal is called an earthdiver and has a special place in the culture of a nation. The earthdiver is usually an animal that is familiar to the Natives: for the Iroquois a muskrat, and for the Cherokee a waterbeetle.

◁▲▽▲▽▲▷ Culture heroes

Culture heroes are particular animals, with human characteristics, who are believed to have been responsible for turning the world into a suitable place for humans to live. In the stories mentioned on the previous pages, the coyote is the culture hero of some Northwestern peoples, for example. Culture heroes shape the landscape, defend the people from monsters, and give the people the basic tools they need to survive.

A famous culture hero is Gluskap, an unselfish hero who figures in the sacred history of Northeastern nations. He killed a monster frog who was causing drought by drinking all the world's water, and ensured that the people had water in order to live.

Tricksters

Other culture heroes were unpredictable, selfish characters, called tricksters. They play a very important part in Native American culture, and often incorporate the positive attributes of the culture hero. Tricksters change the world through their recklessness, but are also often responsible for bringing culture into the world. They get into absurd situations, make people laugh, and clown around.

This wooden bird mask from the Northwest region has an articulated beak.

The trickster animal is the totem animal (see page 35) of a great number of nations. In Plains and mountainous Western regions the trickster is usually a coyote. The raven plays a major role as trickster in the culture of the Northwestern nations, where representations of him abound. The hare also appears as a trickster character in some cultures.

The trickster may appear as half human, half animal. In some Northwestern stories Raven is either partially or entirely human, but wears raven clothes which he can discard to show that he is human. Wooden masks worn for ceremonial occasions may be painted to resemble a human face, but, with the addition of a beak, are wholly raven. In Apache stories, Coyote wears Apache clothes and behaves like a human, even speaking in a human voice, but also runs around on all fours. The blurring of human–animal distinctions is an illustration of the Natives' close relationship with animals.

This Tlingit chief's double-headed fighting knife is carved with a dogfish. It was carried around the neck.

Thunderbird

Thunderbird is a character from sacred history who is wholly animal, resembling a huge eagle. He features as culture hero in many stories, killing monsters to protect his people or catching whales to feed them. He is lord of the skies: thunder is believed to be the roar of his wings, and lightning the flashing of his eyes. He is often represented in the art of Northwestern nations.

Whirlwind

Whirlwind is a character from Sioux sacred history. He is the youngest brother of the four winds, all of whom are sons of Tate, the Wind. Whirlwind is a perpetually playful child who never grew up, and is much loved despite often being naughty. The butterfly, dragonfly, and moth are linked with Whirlwind as their wings produce little eddies of wind. Sioux warriors hope for Whirlwind power in battle – they will be difficult for the enemy to hit, and their twisting, playful movements will confuse him.

Native Americans and Europeans: an historical outline

'They made us many promises, more than I can remember, but they never kept but one; they promised to take our land, and they took it.' **Red Cloud, Oglala Sioux chief**

1528, November • The first Europeans set foot on the American continent at Galveston Island.

1540, July • The first conflict between Europeans and Indians occurs with the Zuni at Hawikuh (Granada).

1620 • Puritans from England arrive on the Atlantic coast.

1775–83 • American Wars of Independence. The US tries to stake its claim to the continent and displaces Northeastern tribes.

1800 • The continent is divided up between several European nations: the US in the east, France from the Mississippi to the Rockies, Spain in the southwest, Britain in the north. Spain sells its Louisiana Territory to France.

1803 • The US buys up the Louisiana Territory from France, so that it now owns half the West.

1813, October 5 • Battle of the Thames, Ontario. Shawnee leader Tecumseh is killed in battle, ending Indian resistance to the US in the midwest.

1819 • The US takes Texas from the Spanish.

1820 • Mexico becomes independent of Spain.

1830, May 28 • US President Andrew Jackson signs the Indian Removal Act, whereby he may make treaties with tribes east of the Mississippi to take their land and give them new territories west of the Mississippi.

1838–9 • The Trail of Tears. As part of the Five Civilized

Tribes' removal to Indian Territory, the Cherokee are forced to walk 1,200 miles during the winter from their homeland to what is now Oklahoma, killing a quarter of them.

1846–8 • War between the US and Mexico, after which the US owns New Mexico and California.

1847 • The US conquers the last Indian nations in California.

1848, January 24 • Discovery of gold at Sutter's Mill, California. The Native population is displaced; 80,000 white men flood across the continent in 1849, killing livestock and crops, and cutting down trees.

1849, Summer • At the Sun Dance ceremony at Smoky Hill River, Kansas, cholera caught from the white population streaming across the continent decimates the Cheyenne, Arapaho, Comanche, Kiowa, and Plains Apache.

1850 • The Department of Indian Affairs decides to divide up Native lands into reservations and ensure Plains nations give up nomadism and warfare.

1851, September • Fort Laramie Treaty. Attended by over 10,000 Cheyenne, Arapaho, Sioux, Crow, Grosventre, Blackfeet, and Shoshone, this is one of the largest gatherings in Indian history. Both sides promise to 'maintain good faith and friendship.'

1854, August • Soldiers open fire at Blue Water Creek, killing 86 Brule Indians and taking 70 women and children. This follows a dispute over a Brule warrior killing a calf from a Mormon wagon that was crossing their land.

1860, April 3 • The first Pony Express mail connects St Joseph, Missouri with Sacramento, California. The US hereby controls the whole continent.

1861–5 • US Civil War. The Five Civilized Tribes in Indian Territory sign up with both North and South armies, leading to civil war within the Territory.

1861 • Fort Wise Treaty. Cheyenne and Arapaho lands are ceded except for a small reservation along Sand Creek.

1862, May 20 • Homestead Act. This encourages people to settle the West by allotting 160 acres to anyone who pays $10, has made a farm, and who works it for five years.

1864, Spring • Navajo Long Walk. More than 8,000 Navajo surrender at their sacred site, Canyon de Chelly, and are made to walk 300 miles to Fort Sumner and the Bosque Redondo, killing hundreds of them. The land they have been allotted there is arid and infertile.

1864, November 29 • Sand Creek Massacre. Despite assurances of safety given to Black Kettle and the Cheyenne, they are attacked, killing 105 women and children, and 28 men. This destroys Black Kettle's hopes of peace. Word of the massacre spreads fast to all Sioux, Arapaho, and Cheyenne, and soon the whole region is at war.

1865 • After the Civil War, nations in Indian Territory who sided with both armies are forced to give up land to other tribes forced to move there from the south.

1866, June • Red Cloud and other Sioux leaders are called to Fort Laramie to discuss a new treaty allowing a road to be built through their sacred lands, the Black Hills and Bighorn Mountains. Red Cloud feels betrayed when he discovers that whites are already being given protection to travel down a road that hasn't yet been built, and calls for war. He and Crazy Horse lead battles.

1867, Late Summer • At Medicine Lodge Creek, Kansas, southern Plains leaders, including Black Kettle, sign an agreement to move onto reservations in present-day Oklahoma in exchange for supplies, schools, and farming help. They don't get their supplies and raid local towns to find food.

1868, June 1 • After 'The fearing time' in the Bosque Redondo, the Navajo are allowed to return to their homeland, onto the largest reservation in the US.

1868, August 13 • The US signs a treaty with the Nez Perce. It is the 370th and last US–Indian treaty.

1868, September • Battle of Beecher's Island, between a US scouting party and Cheyenne and Sioux.

1868, November 6 • Red Cloud finally signs a treaty, already signed by other leaders, agreeing to move onto a vast Sioux reservation. In exchange, the US agrees to abandon its forts in the foothills of the Bighorn Mountains.

Red Cloud (1822–1909) was chief of the Oglala Sioux and a revered holy man.

1868, November 27 • General Custer, with 600 men, attacks the Cheyenne on the Washita River, killing Black Kettle. 6,000 Cheyenne, Arapaho, Kiowa, and Comanche retaliate.

1869, May 10 • The Central Pacific and Union Pacific railroads meet at Promontory Point, Utah, in the first transcontinental railway. The road over which Red Cloud fought in 1866 has been rendered obsolete. Whites begin to make buffalo-shooting expeditions into the Plains.

1870 • The Native population of California has been reduced from 150,000 to 30,000.

1875 • Miners flood to the Black Hills, violating the treaty of 1868. The army is unable to drive them out. Under threats, the US tries to buy or lease the land from the Indians.

1876, Spring • Sitting Bull has a vision of a great dust storm swirling down on a small white cloud resembling a Sioux village. Soldiers march through the whirlwind. The cloud is swallowed up for a while but emerges intact, whereupon the dust storm disappears.

1876, June 6 • At the Sun Dance at Rosebud Creek, Sitting Bull slashes his arm 100 times and has another great vision: Soldiers come to attack his people, but they are upside down with their horses' hooves in the air, their hats tumbling to the ground.

1876, June 17 • Battle of the Rosebud between the US and 500 Sioux and Cheyenne. The Indians hold their own and then move to the Little Bighorn.

1876, June 25 • Battle of the Little Bighorn. Custer and his whole army are killed. This is the greatest Indian victory of the Plains wars, and Sitting Bull is believed to be the Indian who defeated the US army. This is the battle from his visions. In retaliation, the Black Hills are taken from the Indians, and Sitting Bull flees to Canada.

1876, October • Chief Joseph and the Nez Perce are defeated at the Battle of Big Hole and are forced to travel over 1,700 miles to Indian Territory, Oklahoma.

1877, September 5 • Crazy Horse, the last of the great Sioux war chiefs, dies at Fort Robinson, Nebraska, bayoneted in the back. His heart is reputedly buried at Wounded Knee.

1881, July 19 • Sitting Bull comes back from Canada and gives himself up. He and his people are herded onto Standing Rock reservation, hundreds of miles from their home. He is still defiant, but the other chiefs are broken.

1885 • Sitting Bull joins Buffalo Bill's Wild West Show for four months. He has a new vision: Wandering alone near his home one morning he watches a meadowlark flutter down onto a hillock. The bird says that his own people will kill him.

126

1886, September 4 • Geronimo, the Chiricahua Apache leader, surrenders. This is the end of Indian warfare in the US.

1890, December 15 • Kicking Bear brings a version of the Ghost Dance religion (see page 52) to Sitting Bull, who encourages the inhabitants of Standing Rock to go to the dance. Sioux policemen try to stop Sitting Bull from leaving, and he ends up shot. His grieving followers are joined by Big Foot and the Miniconjous, who travel to Wounded Knee, South Dakota.

1890, December 29 • Battle of Wounded Knee. The Sioux are massacred in the snow. This ends disturbances among the Western Indians that were caused by the Ghost Dance religion .

1891, January 15 • 4,000 Ghost Dancers, including 1,000 warriors, give themselves up.

1900 • There are only 237,000 Native Americans left, the smallest number since the European settlers landed on the continent.

Each eagle tail feather in this war bonnet signifies a specific war honor won by the owner.

'I did not know then how much was ended. When I look back now from this high hill of my old age, I can still see the butchered women and children lying heaped and scattered all along the crooked gulch as plain as when I saw them with eyes still young. And I can see that something else died there in the bloody mud, and was buried in the blizzard. A people's dream died there. It was a beautiful dream... the nation's hoop is broken and scattered. There is no center any longer, and the sacred tree is dead.' **Black Elk, Oglala Sioux visionary, and witness to the Battle of Wounded Knee**

FURTHER READING

Dee Brown, *Bury My Heart at Wounded Knee: An Indian History of the American West*, Vintage, London, 1991

Joseph Epes Brown, ed., *The Sacred Pipe: Black Elk's Account of the Seven Rites of the Oglala Sioux*, Penguin, New York, 1971

Joseph Epes Brown, *Animals of the Soul: Sacred Animals of the Oglala Sioux*, Element, Shaftesbury, 1992

J.C. Cooper, *Dictionary of Symbolic and Mythological Animals*, Thorsons, London, 1992

Paula Richardson Fleming and Judith Luskey, *The North American Indians in Early Photographs*, Phaidon, London, 1988

Daniel Francis, *Copying People: Photographing British Columbia First Nations, 1860–1940*, Fifth House, Saskatoon and Calgary, 1996

Alvin M. Josephy, Jr, *500 Nations: An Illustrated History of the North American Indians*, Hutchinson/Pimlico, London, 1995

J. Neihardt, ed., *Black Elk Speaks*, Pocket, New York, 1972

David W. Penney, *Art of the American Indian Frontier*, Phaidon, London, 1992

Lewis Spence, *The Myths of the North American Indians*, Dover, New York, 1989

Colin F. Taylor, *Native American Life: The Family, The Hunt, Pastimes and Ceremonies*, Salamander, London, 1996

Arthur Versluis, *The Elements of Native American Traditions*, Element, Shaftesbury, 1993

Geoffrey C. Ward, *The West: An Illustrated History*, Weidenfeld & Nicolson, London, 1996

Larry J. Zimmerman, *Native North America: Belief and Ritual, Visionaries, Holy People and Tricksters, Spirits of Earth and Sky*, Duncan Baird, London, 1996

ACKNOWLEDGEMENTS

The publishers would like to thank the following sources for their kind permission to reproduce the pictures in this book:

Corbis-Bettmann: 19, 112, 120 /Robert Estall 117, Werner Forman Archive/British Museum, London 127, Field Museum of Natural History, Chicago 121, Museum of the American Indian, Heye Foundation, NY 29, Plains Indian Museum Buffalo Bill History Center, Cody, Wyoming USA 12, 17, Smithsonian Institution, Washington D.C. 108, Peter Newark's Western Americana: 10, 25, 115, 125.

Every effort has been made to acknowledge correctly and contact the source and copyright holder of each picture, and Carlton Books Limited apologizes for any unintentional errors or omissions which will be corrected in future editions of this book.